HITLER'S HEADQUARTERS

Other Books by Blaine Taylor

Guarding the Führer:
Sepp Dietrich, Johann Rattenhuber and the Protection of Adolf Hitler (1993)

Fascist Eagle: Italy's Air Marshal Italo Balbo (1996)

Mercedes-Benz Parade and Staff Cars of the Third Reich (1999)

Volkswagen Military Vehicles of the Third Reich (2004)

Apex of Glory: Mercedes-Benz, 1885–1955 (2006)

HITLER'S HEADQUARTERS
FROM BEER HALL TO BUNKER, 1920–1945

Blaine Taylor

Potomac Books, Inc.
Washington, D.C.

Library of Congress Cataloging-in-Publication Data
Taylor, Blaine, 1946–
  Hitler's headquarters : from beer hall to bunker, 1920–1945 / Blaine Taylor. — 1st ed.
    p. cm.
  Includes bibliographical references and index.
  ISBN-13: 978-1-57488-928-4 (hardcover : alk. paper)
  1. Hitler, Adolf, 1889–1945—Homes and haunts. 2. Heads of state—Germany—
Homes and haunts. 3. Germany—Armed Forces—Headquarters—History. I. Title.
  DD247.H5T344 2007
  943.086—dc22

                              2006034981

ISBN-13: 978-1-57488-928-4

(alk. paper)

Printed in the United States of America on acid-free paper that meets the American National Standards Institute Z39-48 Standard.

Potomac Books, Inc.
22841 Quicksilver Drive
Dulles, Virginia 20166

First Edition

10 9 8 7 6 5 4 3 2 1

Dedicated to

James F. Waesche—former Baltimore *Sun*
writer, editor of *Baltimore Magazine,* and
President of the Society of the War of 1812
in Maryland—and current publisher of
*The Blue Book of Roland Park, Guilford,
Homeland and Several Adjacent Areas.*
Mentor, good, honest man, friend,
and the first person to pay me what
the job was actually worth.

"He never used a desk but to sit on it," asserted an associate, but here Adolf Hitler poses for a formal shot in his Brown House Nazi Party headquarters office in Munich. *HHA*

CONTENTS

ACKNOWLEDGMENTS

First to be thanked are editor Don Jacobs and publisher Don McKeon of Potomac Books for agreeing to undertake this project. Next come the entire staffs of the various photographic source museums and archives of the U.S. government, with whom I began working in the fall of 1967 on all my illustrated book projects immediately after I left the military during the later part of the Vietnam War.

I'd also like to thank ace photography consultant Stan Piet of Bel Air, who has worked with me on all of my books since 1992; German translator Mrs. Erika Burke of Glen Burnie, aboard for the last three; computer consultant Frank White of Parkville; and both William Seim and David Whitely of Ritz Camera of Towson (all of Maryland), who have produced excellent photographic results for the last several of my books.

I thank, too, mentor P. James Kurapka of Gate City, Virginia, and agent Capt. William Hancock, USA (Ret.), USMA, West Point, class of 1971, of Darien, Connecticut.

The late superb researcher and writer on all things FHQ—Richard Raiber, MD, of Hockessin, Delaware—regrettably passed away on March 28, 2002, according to his son Thomas. Thus, he will not be able to critique this book upon publication as he did my first one in 1993. In this field, there was no one better; a harsh but accurate critic generally, he both was and remains the very best.

Finally, I wish to thank tireless researcher Joseph Eagan of the Enoch Pratt Free Library in Baltimore and Mrs. Joan Lattanzi of the Baltimore County Public Library's interlibrary loan system in Towson. Both aided me greatly in acquiring rare articles and books on the period discussed in this work. Of special help on FHQ Kasino Hotel Zoppot was John H. Bloecher, Jr., of the Danzig Study Group in Baltimore.

As with anything else, this book is the sum of its many parts, and all of the above-mentioned people played vital roles in the production of the work that follows.

Unless otherwise credited, all of the photographs in this book are from the following major sources: the Hermann Göring Albums at the Library of Congress, Washington, D.C.; the Eva Braun Hitler, Joachim von Ribbentrop, and Heinrich Hoffmann Albums; and Captured Enemy Records, all in the U.S. National Archives, College Park, Maryland.

INTRODUCTION
FROM WHENCE THE REICH WAS RULED AND THE WAR WAS WAGED

The year was 1943, the site, German Army Field Marshal Fritz Erich von Manstein's headquarters in the Nazi-occupied Union of Soviet Socialist Republics (USSR). He was awaiting an important visitor: Führer and Reich Chancellor Adolf Hitler, his commander in chief.

The field marshal's aide, Alexander von Stahlberg, was also present, and he left an account in his postwar work *Bounden Duty: Memoirs of a German Officer, 1932–45.*

> **Something unusual . . . a large, dark-colored wooden chest, was moving towards us from the staircase. It must have measured about a cubic meter, with handles at the four corners. Four SS men were carrying it, with a fifth walking ahead, who asked the Field Marshal and onlookers to stand aside for a moment to allow the closet to pass.**
>
> **Then the fifth man opened the doors to the lavatories . . . the bearers and their burden disappeared into that sweet-smelling area of the top floor. When the door shut again, Manstein asked Gen. [Rudolf] Schmundt, "What on earth was that?"**
>
> **Schmundt told him—rather awkwardly— that it was the Führer's new dry closet.**

British revisionist historian David Irving stated in his 1977 work, *Hitler's War,* that his purpose was to show how things looked from behind the Führer's desk—at which he rarely, if ever, sat. "He used a desk only to sit on," recalled an associate, and thus his decisions in both peace and war were made from wherever Hitler happened to be at the time: an outdoor café, at the opera, in his various private and official residences, and later from his rustic, wooded, Camp David–style military Führer Headquarters, or FHQ, which also included his special train on at least two major occasions during World War II.

To purists—as the late preeminent authority Richard Raiber, MD—the term *FHQ* (or, more precisely from the German, FHQu) referred only to the wartime military Führer Headquarters during 1939–45. In actuality, the FHQs housed Hitler and OKW (High Command of the Armed Forces), as well as the various services' liaison officers to the Führer, plus his aides and adjutants from both the Party and the state. OKH (High Command of the Army), OKM (Navy), and OKL (Air Force) were but invited guests to FHQ, and often they were even located many miles away from it. As Alfred Jodl stated in his unpublished diary, "It was hard to be an 'invited guest' for 5 ½ years."

In this work, I have expanded the coverage of the wartime FHQs of 1939–45 to include all of Hitler's private residences and political Nazi Party and German State FHQs from where he conceived first his design to take over republican Germany; next, his diplomatic moves to acquire territory peacefully; and finally, his plans to wage war when he could achieve no more through peaceful means. Indeed, each led from one to the next: Hitler's prewar military planning to avenge imperial Germany's loss of World War I began from his cot in the hospital room of a military medical facility, and he pursued his vengeance from all other FHQ locations.

Exactly how each of these sites played a part in the prewar and wartime periods is demonstrated herein. Without the former, there would never have been the latter. Thus, this work concentrates on the "where" and the "what" of these sites and structures, as well as two basic questions concerning them: What did the FHQs look like, inside and out? and What was it like to actually live in one for days, weeks, months, and even years at a time?

No other politico-military commander in history—for Hitler, just as Napoleon I, was both—had as many command posts as the Führer did, and yet they were still not enough. Indeed, until the last days of the war, more were being built: bigger, better, and far more costly to boot. Their expense in money, time, talent, and material was a major factor in Nazi Germany losing World War II, although Hitler and the Nazis fully expected to win it, even up to the spring of 1945, with the Third Reich invaded from both east and west. From a military standpoint, the war was hopelessly lost, but they still sought a politically victorious end.

The very year that Albert Speer presented Hitler with the sumptuous, New German Reich Chancellery in Berlin—1939—the latter was already planning for 1950, when his total victory over a Nazi-dominated world would be celebrated from his rebuilt global capital, Germania (the former, far more modest Berlin of the Kaisers). Rudolf Hess was to be given the "new" Chancellery, and Hitler would reign over the earth from the Führer Palace instead.

But it didn't work out that way, and the places where the decisions were made that led to the failure of this vision are the very core of the following saga of bricks and mortar, wood and concrete, iron and steel.

ABBREVIATIONS

BFP: Billy F. Price
CER: Captured Enemy Records, National Archives
CP: Command Post
DSG: Danzig Study Group
FHQ: Führer Headquarters
HGA: Hermann Göring Albums
HHA: Heinrich Hoffmann Albums
HST: Harry S. Truman Library
JRA: Joachim von Ribbentrop Albums
LC: Library of Congress
New RC: New Reich Chancellery Berlin
OKH: Oberkommando des Heeres (High Command of the Army)
OKL: Oberkommando der Luftwaffe (High Command of the Air Force)

OKM: Oberkommando der Kriegsmarine (High Command of the Navy)
Old RC: Old Reich Chancellery Berlin
OT: Organization Todt
RCA: Ray Cowdery Archives
RFSS: Reichsführer SS/SS National Administrator (Himmler)
RSD: Reichssicherheitsdienstm (Reich Security Service, detectives in uniform)
SC: U.S. Army Signal Corps
SS: Security Service
USNA: U.S. National Archives
WFSt: Wehrmachtführungsstab/OKW Operations Staff (Wehrmacht/Armed Forces High Command, formed in 1935)

HOSPITAL ROOM TO BROWN HOUSE TO BERLIN, 1918–1933

In 1913, prior to World War I, Adolf Hitler moved from Austria across the border into neighboring Germany to Munich, Bavaria, in order to avoid the Austrian draft—allegedly because he did not want to serve in the racially mixed Imperial Austrian Army. Another story, however, suggested that he was found unfit for duty (too weak to bear arms) at a medical checkup for service at Salzburg.

No, if Hitler were going to serve in the military, he preferred to do it in Germany. When war broke out, the Germans were glad to have him because they needed soldiers. After serving honorably throughout World War I, the wounded, almost-blinded Hitler decided to enter politics because the armistice enraged him. He moved back to Munich. By stages, he eventually became the leader (Führer) of the tiny Nazi Party, the early headquarters of which were the public beer halls or large taverns where meetings were held.

Hitler's First Rented Room in Munich

Hitler's first rented room in Munich was at Schleissheimerstrasse #34, on the third floor above the ground-level Josef Popp Tailor Shop. Hitler arrived from Austria on May 25, 1913, and shared the room until mid-February 1914 with Rudolf Hausler. After that, he lived there alone until the war broke out the following August. Hitler paid the rent by painting and selling architectural watercolors door-to-door and in the local beer halls. His landlady recalled that he had no visitors at all for the year and a half that he rented there.

Soldier for the Second Reich

On August 2, 1914, Hitler was among the throng that sang "Watch on the Rhine" and "Germany Over All" on the city's Odeonsplatz to celebrate the coming world war. He soon wrote to Bavarian King Ludwig III, asking to be accepted into the Royal Bavarian Army as an Austrian volunteer; he was.

Rather than returning to Austria, Hitler was allowed to volunteer for the First Bavarian (List) Infantry Regiment on August 5, 1914, and was ordered to report for duty on the sixteenth for training. Decades later in his Berlin bunker, Hitler dated what he called his service to his people for the three Germanies—imperial, republican (as a foe), and Nazi—from May 25, 1913, through April 30, 1945, the day of his death.

He served for four years as a soldier and a messenger in his infantry regiment on the Western Front, where he was wounded. The last time, he was temporarily blinded by mustard gas and sent to a military hospital at Pasewalk, Pomerania, in Germany to recover. By November 11, Hitler had heard that the ruling dynasties had fallen, that revolution had broken out, and that an armistice with the Allies had been signed that ended the war in defeat for Germany. It was here, in his own hospital room, that rebellious Red Communist sailors burst in to recruit for the revolution that was sweeping Germany during November 1918.

In the wake of the German government's declaration of a republic, former artist and would-be architect Adolf Hitler made the most fateful decision of his life from his hospital bed. As he wrote later in *Mein Kampf* (My Battle): "I resolved that—if I recovered my sight—I would enter politics." And he did, on both counts. Thus, this room was, in a very real sense, Hitler's first peacetime FHQ. On November 19, 1918, Hitler was discharged from the hospital and traveled home to Munich via Berlin, where he witnessed the ongoing Red revolution of the Soldiers' and Sailors' Councils firsthand. It has even been suggested that Hitler turned first to the German Left and the Communists for a place in their party, but was rejected.

Back in Munich on the twenty-first, Gefreiter (Private First Class) Hitler, age twenty-nine, was housed in the Army barracks at Lothstrasse #29 as a member of the First Reserve Battalion, Second Infantry Regiment (Hitler was never a corporal in the American sense with two stripes; he had but one). Meanwhile, a Communist government ruled the city of Munich and the state of Bavaria from November 1918 through May 1919, almost seven months. This period is the murkiest of his life, in that it is not known to which side he really belonged—the Left or the Right.

In May 1919, German conservative rightist forces overthrew the Communists in a bloody counterrevolution. This event persuaded Hitler that he must seek his hoped-for political activity there. He had been a gate sentry and also pulled guard duty at a municipal railroad station. He had even tested old gas masks for extra pay. In June, Hitler was assigned as a right-wing political lecturer to the troops, and it was then he developed the talent that made him one of the greatest political orators in history.

Gefreiter Hitler could have remained in the Army until he retired, but he made a second great postwar decision: he asked to be discharged from the Army, which had been his steady home for five years and eight months, and headed for the uncertainty of a life in politics as an unknown war veteran among millions.

Hitler's Second Rented Room in Munich

Gathering his meager belongings, which consisted of a cap, coat, jacket, trousers, underwear, shirt, socks, shoes, and demobilization pay of but fifty marks, Hitler moved to a small room at Thierschstrasse #41 on March 31, 1920. It would be his home for the next nine years.

He arrived at this room—sublet from a Jew—as an unknown person and left it as a national political figure. Visitor Ernst Hanfstaengl described the room in his 1957 work *Unheard Witness* as such:

> **Drab and dreary beyond belief, akin to a back bedroom of a decaying New York tenement. The room . . . was tiny. I doubt it was nine feet wide. The bed was too wide for its corner, and the head projected over a single narrow window. The floor was covered with cheap, worn linoleum with a couple of threadbare rugs, and on the wall opposite the bed there was a makeshift bookshelf, apart from the chair and rough table, the only other piece of furniture in the entire room.**

It was also the house's coldest room. Hitler's landlady later said that he paid the rent either on time or in advance, and he kept his German shepherd dog, Wolf, as company. Today, the building still stands with a statue of the Virgin Mary staring down from an alcove on the second floor's outer wall. The room itself, however, was known to make later tenants ill, and since no one would rent it anymore, it was turned into a storeroom.

The Nazi Party and Beer Halls

The so-called birthplace of the Nazi Party and its first office was the Sterneckerbräu (brewery, or beer hall) at Tal # 54–55 (or #38 in some accounts). Here, on September 12, 1919, Gefreiter Hitler became Member #555 of the German Workers' Party (DAP), the meetings of which he had been ordered to attend undercover as a spy. When the new National Socialist German Workers' (Nazi) Party was formed early in 1920, Hitler became Member #7.

The meeting didn't impress Hitler, but he was given a brochure titled "My Political Awakening" by founder Anton Drexler, and he read it nonetheless. Hitler was invited to the next DAP meeting at the Altes Rosenbad Inn and his Intelligence Division superior, Capt. Karl Mayr, again ordered him to attend and even join the tiny party.

After joining, Hitler was said to have established an office there in a former barroom with a light, telephone, table, a few chairs on loan, a bookcase, and borrowed cupboards. Thus was born what would become the first FHQ of the future Nazi Party, a party Hitler would change in name, direction, and leadership.

In addition to being an excellent speaker before mass audiences, Hitler was a gifted organizer and motivator. He created brochures, banners, slogans, and flags, and he was a superb strategist and able tactician. Hitler turned a seven-member party into one attracting millions and headed the government of one of Central Europe's most educated and powerful states—a feat unheard of in modern political history.

In 1920, the Party rented the Sterneckerbräu's backroom for its first political headquarters. Hitler described it in *Mein Kampf* as "a small, vaulted room. On overcast days, everything was dark. We brightened the walls with posters announcing our meetings, and for the first time hung up our new flag." Along with those posters, the party's first propogandist, Hitler, designed the red-white-and-black nationalist colors of the swastika banner.

Party annals later bestowed the dramatic name *Kampfzeit* (time of struggle) on the Nazi Party's genesis period of 1920–33. From its official founding on February 24, 1920, it took a little more than twelve years for Hitler to become Reich chancellor of the German government on January 30, 1933.

In the interim were lean years for the Nazis—years of beer hall brawls and pitched street battles, mainly with members of the rival German Communist Party; run-ins with the law; and hotly contested electoral campaigns at local, provincial, and national levels to elect Nazi Party candidates to office. Still, these conflicts were crucial to Hitler for gaining publicity, members, money, and power in his struggle to attain national office for himself and the Nazi Party.

Even today, Munich's illustrious Hofbräuhaus is known as "the most famous beer hall in the world." The DAP—the future Nazi Party—held its first mass meeting there on October 16, 1919, or less than a year after the war's end, with an audience of seventy people. On February 24, 1920, this time with two thousand in attendance in its Festival Hall, Hitler presented the Twenty-five Points that formed the political base of the Nazi Party. (Members came to be called Nazis, an abbreviation of the Party's full name, just as the Socialists were called Sozis.) After the audience heard the Twenty-five Points and approved them all—one after the other—the pivotal meeting ended. "The Movement took its course," recalled Hitler.

On August 13, 1920, Hitler publicly denounced the Jews and demanded their removal from Germany altogether. On November 4, 1921, during a massive fight between the Nazis and their opponents in the Hofbräuhaus, Hitler managed to complete another address, despite the chaos of smashed tables and chairs and hurled beer mugs all about him.

The Hofbräuhaus was also the birthplace of the feared Nazi street fighting organization, the Sturmabteilungen (Storm Troops, named after World War I German Army shock forces), or SA for short.

The Löwenbräukeller beer hall was located at Nymphenburgerstrasse #4 on Stiglmaier Plaza in Munich. Hitler commanded the SA to break up a meeting of the rival Bavarian League there on September 14, 1921. He also ordered the SA to assault its main speaker, Otto Ballerstedt.

On November 8–9, 1923, at Munich's Bürgerbräukeller beer hall, Hitler attempted to seize first that city, then Bavaria, and finally the Reich by force, just as Benito "the Duce" Mussolini had done in Italy almost exactly a year before; Hitler, however, failed miserably. Following that abysmal debacle, Hitler decided that in the future he would gain office only through legal means. A decade later, he replaced the old state with a new Nazi model that he and the Party had built up during the intervening ten years.

On February 27, 1925, Hitler made his first major public address at the Bürgerbräukeller to an overall crowd of five thousand people. He had refounded the previously banned Nazi Party the day before.

In 1939, the Führer cut short his putsch commemorative speech in the same hall and left just before an explosion killed or wounded several Party members—an event still not entirely explained. Following the destruction of the Bürgerbräukeller by would-be assassin Georg Elser's bomb blast on November 8, 1939, the Führer and others honored the anniversary of the 1923 Bürgerbräukeller Putsch at the Löwenbräukeller throughout the rest of the war.

On November 9, 1943, the Führer celebrated the twentieth anniversary of the Bürgerbräukeller Putsch with a speech before the Nazi Party Old Fighters at the Löwenbräukeller. In addition to the dead of 1923, Hitler added the commemoration of the casualties of the war from 1939–43, hoping to shore up support for himself, the Party, the regime, and the war in Munich—the vaunted "Capital of the Movement." Reflecting wartime realities, Hitler sent

Col. Gen. Alfred Jodl to speak in his stead, a soldier in place of a revolutionary.

The 1944 anniversary meeting was held, instead of at the Bürgerbräukeller, at the Circus Krone in Munich and was addressed by Heinrich Himmler. While one account states that Himmler read Hitler's address for him on November 8, 1944, another asserts that the event was cancelled instead. Bombed later in 1944, it became a food warehouse and was looted in 1945. Then it burned down in 1986 before being rebuilt.

During 1945–57, the Bürgerbräukeller was a U.S. Army beer hall for Occupation troops. From 1957 to 1979, it became a public drinking house once more, after which it was torn down to make way for a new Hilton Hotel.

Corneliusstrasse #12 housed the Café Gastotte. It was the second Nazi Party headquarters (now gone) in Munich during the 1923 Bürgerbräukeller Putsch, which was organized at Schellingstrasse #50.

The third Nazi Party headquarters in Munich was at Thierschstrasse #15 in "a room in the premises of the publishers Franz Eher & Successors when the Führer refounded the Party on February 27, 1925," according to Dr. Adolf Dresler in his article "The Brown House." It was abandoned sometime before Hitler became chancellor on January 30, 1933.

Schellingstrasse #39 was the Munich street address for the offices of the Party's official newspaper, the *People's Observer*, edited by Alfred Rosenberg. It was also the SA's headquarters before and during the 1923 Bürgerbräukeller Putsch, at which time it became a command post (CP).

Schellingstrasse #50 was, during 1925–31, the fourth Nazi Party headquarters in Munich. It had several rooms in the rear of the building. The front housed Heinrich Hoffmann's photographic studio, where the Führer met shop assistant Eva Braun in October 1929.

Schellingstrasse #56 housed the Schelling-Salon restaurant, close to the Hoffmann studio. It was the Party's headquarters as well as the home of the *People's Observer*, for a time. Hitler left it when his credit was stopped!

Hitler as Jailbird

Following the failure of the Bürgerbräukeller Putsch, the future Führer was jailed at Blutenburgstrasse #18 in Munich in a holding cell while awaiting trial for treason during 1923–24. Most readers are familiar with Hitler's time in prison following the famous putsch, but few know that he had previously been convicted and received a five-month sentence beginning on June 4, 1922, for inciting a riot. He had served this sentence at Munich's Stadelheim prison, where—twelve years later—Hitler had

Ernst Röhm and several other dissident SA leaders shot for alleged treason against the state.

Following his conviction at the Bürgerbräukeller Putsch trial, Hitler served nine months of a five-year prison term during 1924 at the Bavarian fortress of Landsberg am Lech (River), forty miles west of Munich. Hitler entered the fortress with a dislocated left shoulder and a broken upper arm after he fell under police gunfire as the putsch was crushed.

During Hitler's imprisonment, he and his fellow Nazi inmates all wore their own clothes and even had beer! It was at Landsberg that Hitler and Hess began writing *Mein Kampf* and where Hitler also recast all his former ideas about political issues, the Party's organization, and what he wanted to do when he took office. He used the time to educate himself as well, reading history books and the writings of Lenin, Schopenhauer, and Clausewitz. Because of his war record and the secret popularity of his party even among some of his judges, Hitler was released early for good behavior. Ironically, the same prison housed convicted Nazi war criminals after World War II, and some were also hanged there.

Following his release from Landsberg, Hitler decided to establish his next personal headquarters on the Obersalzberg, not far from Munich.

Cafés and Coffeehouses

While frequenting cafés, coffeehouses, salons, and beer halls, Hitler both launched his political career and found his most ardent followers. Back in Munich, the outdoor Café Heck at the corner of Gallery and Ludwigstrasse, looking toward the famous English Gardens, was where Hitler and his inner circle sat at reserved tables and discussed politics, both before and after he became Reich chancellor. He also worked on *Mein Kampf* there. Another favorite haunt was the Café Weichard next to the People's Theater. The Café Neumayr was at Petersplatz #8, just south of St. Peter's Church in Munich, and where the young Hitler went to Monday night gatherings to sound out his associates on various new political ideas in the early 1920s.

Hitler's Third Residence in Munich and Only Apartment

Prinzregentenplatz #16—the Führer's third and final Munich city dwelling—was a nine-room apartment on the second floor above the ground floor. His niece and alleged lover, Angela "Geli" Raubal, died there on September 17, 1931, under mysterious circumstances. Hitler also met with Mussolini there on September 25, 1937.

During their hour-long summit conference, the German and Fascist Italian leaders agreed to continue supporting Gen. Francisco Franco in Spain, to seek better relations with imperial Japan, and to oppose Franco-

British policies that prevented their joint expansion of power and territorial acquisitions. Thus they strengthened the Axis Pact of 1935 and the Anti-Comintern (Communist International) Pact of 1936.

On September 30, 1938, Hitler hosted British Prime Minister Neville Chamberlain at the apartment following the signing of the four-power Munich Pact and before the signing of the Anglo-German declaration that led Chamberlain to declare that he had brought "peace for our time" home with honor from Germany.

As for Hitler, he later boasted to his intimates: "I saw our enemies at Munich—they are little worms!" Because of the document signed in Hitler's apartment, Chamberlain mistakenly thought they'd guaranteed European peace for a generation. Nazi Germany occupied the German Südetenland—taken from the Czechs—the next day.

The Brown House in Munich

The Brown House was located at Briennerstrasse #45 in Munich, and it was the Nazi Party headquarters during 1929–45. The former three-story, neo-classical Barlow Palace, dating from 1828 and in the plain Biedermeier style common in those times, was renamed the Brown House (for the color of the SA uniforms) in 1931. It had once been the former Italian legation, and the Nazis converted the building's attics into another story.

Architect Dr. Paul Ludwig Troost did the renovation. Hitler's bodyguard chief Sepp Dietrich had a room there, and sometimes the Führer stayed overnight. From the Brown House, Hitler executed his plans for the political conquest of Germany during 1929–33.

During 1933–35, a tunnel reportedly was built connecting the Brown House with the nearby Führerbau (Leader Building), and it was from the Brown House that Hitler went by car to arrest Röhm and the other dissident SA leaders on the "Night of the Long Knives," June 30, 1934.

Inside the Führer's second-floor office was a bust of Mussolini, red-brown walls, and high windows (a future typical room feature) looking out on the Königsplatz (King's Plaza), which still exists today. Peter Adam in *Art of the Third Reich* noted, "The standard for future Party buildings was set here . . . much earnest wood paneling on walls and ceiling . . . a vast staircase led to Hitler's office, with its portrait of Frederick the Great over a large desk. There were also pictures of Prussian battles . . . a Senate chamber was constructed . . . 60 chairs in red leather, with swastikas on their backs for 60 Senators around a vast conference table."

A Nazi Senate never met, however, as the Führer feared being voted out of Party office by such a body—as had happened to Mussolini in 1943 with the Fascist Grand Council in Rome. Dr. Otto Dietrich recalled in his memoir, *Hitler*, "The Party Senate—which Hitler had promised to form and for which the Senate Hall in the Brown House at

Munich had been completely furnished—never came into existence. Decisions were made by Hitler alone, then passed on to the government and the Party as accomplished facts. Having announced his decrees, Hitler declared that they were essential to the welfare of the nation."

The Führer often ate his meals in the Brown House canteen with brown-shirted SA men seated on rustic Bavarian chairs. Besides Hitler's own office on the second floor, there were also those of the SA chief of staff, the Party treasurer, and the Party administration. Hitler spent little time there, though, preferring instead to carry on Party business at his usual café and eatery haunts.

The Brown House was greatly damaged by British Royal Air Force (RAF) bombs on March 9–10, 1943. By the time of its fall to the U.S. Army in 1945, it was a mere shell of its former self.

The Hotel Kaiserhof in Berlin

On October 12, 1930, all 107 newly elected Nazi members of the national parliament (the Reichstag) met at the Kaiserhof after their big electoral victory to declare anew their fealty to Hitler as Führer.

During 1932–33, Hitler switched the major focus of his political activities from the Bavarian capital of Munich to the seat of government at Berlin. He set up shop at the Hotel Kaiserhof on Wilhelmstrasse, directly across the street from his ultimate goal: the Old Reich Chancellery building.

By choosing the Kaiserhof (Imperial Court) as his national and political FHQ in Berlin, Hitler was serving notice to friends and foes alike that he was both serious and there to stay. Dr. Paul Josef Göbbels even wrote a book about the Party's final surge to office called *From Kaiserhof to Reich Chancellery*. In January 1932, Hitler rented the entire second floor for his suite, and thus he could see his own future offices from his hotel window. Dr. Göbbels recalled, "The most urgent conferences are held on the stairs, in the hall, at the door, or on the way to the station."

It was at the Kaiserhof on March 18, 1932, that the Führer made his historic decision to campaign for the German presidency by airplane from city to city, giving several major addresses daily under the slogan "Hitler Over Germany." During this campaign he came to employ Hans Baur as his personal pilot until the end in 1945.

A major Nazi Party caucus was held at the hotel on September 6, 1932, after the Nazis became the strongest party in the Prussian state legislature the previous April. Three months later, in July, the Party obtained the same stature in the national Reichstag by winning 230 deputy seats and became the dominant force in that body as well. Within one hundred days, Hitler was appointed—not elected—chancellor.

Hitler held court daily in the Hotel Kaiserhof's famed café during 1932–33. In this period he held intense political negotiations with conservative right-wing politicians to persuade the very man who had defeated him twice for the presidency, Field Marshal Paul von Hindenburg, to name Hitler the Reich chancellor.

According to William L. Shirer in *The Rise and Fall of the Third Reich*, on January 30, the historic day of his appointment as chancellor, following the short ceremony with von Hindenburg across the street at the Old Reich Chancellery. Hitler crowed to his waiting lieutenants at the Kaiserhof, "We've done it!"

(Above) A self-portrait of Adolf Hitler as a common Imperial German Army infantryman in World War I, complete with an oversized Iron Cross (which he was awarded in both the First and Second Classes), and the 1914–16 spiked helmet. This illustration appeared atop a short letter to his first Munich landlord, Josef Popp. *BFP*

Overleaf: A 1938 map of Munich showing many of Hitler's haunts in the city center. In particular, see the Sterneckerbräu (11), the Bürgerbräukeller (16), the Hofbräuhaus (22), the Führerbau (46), and the Brown House (48). *Ray and Josephine Cowdery Archive*

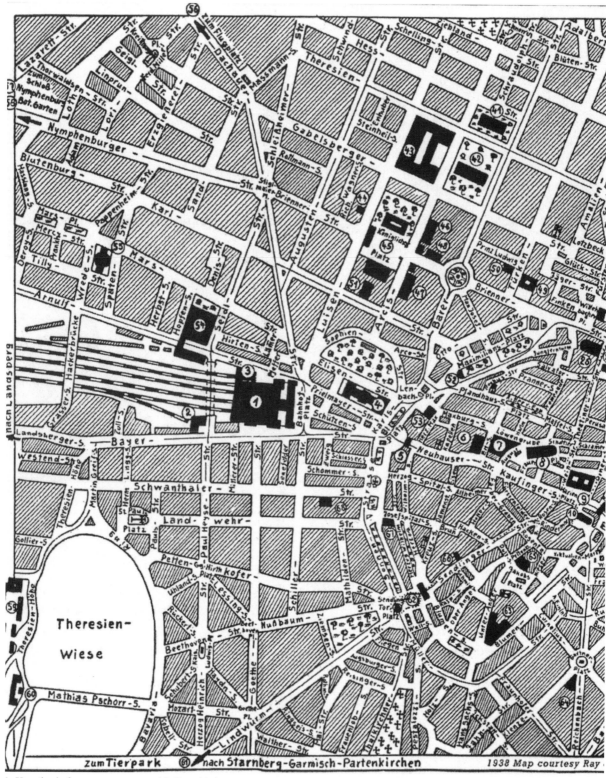

1 Hauptbanhof	10 Peterskirche	18 Alpines Museum	26 Theatinerkirche
2 Hoizkirchner Bahnhof	11 Sterneckberbräu	19 Bayer.Soz.Landesmuseum	27 Odeon
3 Starnberger Bahnhof	Gebburtsstat der NSDAP	20 Ständige Kunstaussteilung	28 Armeemuseum, Kriegerdk.
4 Justizpalast	12 Isator	und Völkerkundemuseum	29 Marstallmuseum
5 Karlstor	13 Deutsches Museum	21 Schauspielhaus	30 Haus der Deutschen Kunst
6 Michaelskirche	14 Vater Rhein-Brunnen	22 Hofbräuhaus	31 Nationalmuseum
7 Polizeidirekt., Fremdenamt	15 Städt. Volksbad	23 Staatstheater	32 Schackgalerie
8 Frauenkirche, Dom	16 Bürgenbräukeller	24 Residenzmuseum	33 Prinzregententheater
9 Neues und Altes Rathaus	17 Maximilianeum	25 Reidhernhalle	34 Chineslscher Turm

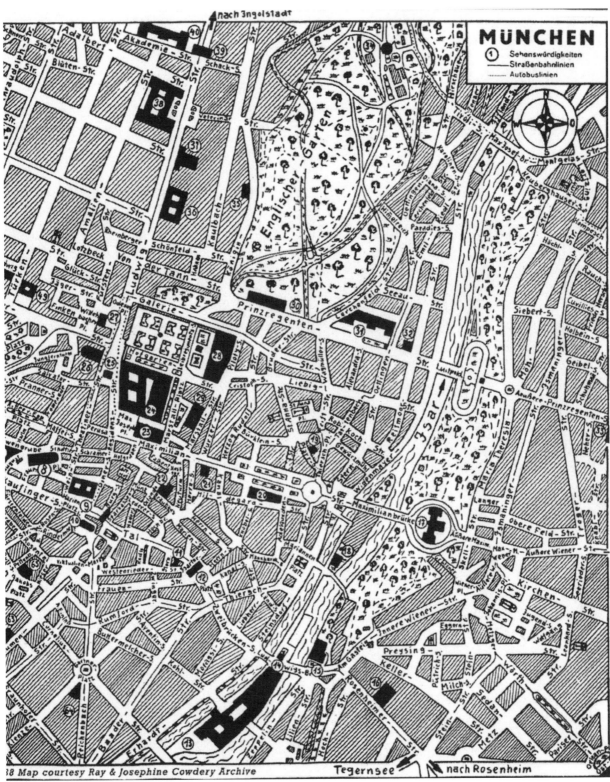

8 Map courtesy Ray & Josephine Cowdery Archive

35 Theatermuseum	44 Lenbachgalerie, Städt. Gal.	52 Wiltelsbacher Brunnen	61 Tierpark
36 Staatsbibliothek	45 Königl.Platz.m.Propylaen	53 Künstlerhaus	62 Sendlinger Tor
37 Ludwigskirche	Staatsgalerie u. Glyptothek	54 Verkehrsministerialgebd.	63 Technisches Rathaus
38 Universität	46 Führerbau	55 Zirkus Krone	64 Gärtnerplatzheater
39 Siegestor	47 Verwaltungsbäude	56 Flugplatz	65 Historisches Stadtmuseum
40 Akademie der Kunste	48 Braunes Haus	57 Schloß Nymphenburg	66 Johan-Nepomuk-Kirche
41 Neue Pinakothek	49 Wittelschacher Palais	58 Staatl. Botanischer Garten	67 Volkstheater
42 Alta Pinakothek	50 Tonhalle	59 Ausstellungsgelände	68 Deutsches Theater
43 Technische Hochschule	51 Basilika	60 Bavaria mit Ruhmeschalle	

(Left) Schleissheimerstrasse #34, Hitler's first rented room in Munich, was on the third floor above a tailor shop. He lived there from May 25, 1913, until August 16, 1914, when he enlisted in the German Army for service in World War I. *HHA*

(Right) Master Tailor Josef Popp's shop had a Nazi plaque above it during the Third Reich (center) that read, "Adolf Hitler lived here from the spring of 1912 [*sic*] until he volunteered for military service in August 1914." During World War I, Gefreiter Hitler wrote home regularly to "Dear Herr Popp." The plaque was removed in 1945. *HHA*

(Right) Hitler's second rented room in Munich was in the building at Thierschstrasse #41, March 1920–October 1929. *Steven Lehrer, Hitler Sites: A City-by-City Guidebook, by permission of McFarland & Company*

(Above) The doorway to Hitler's room at the military hospital in Pasewalk, commemorated by the plaque above the door (placed in 1933). *HHA*

(Left) Inside Hitler's shared hospital room, his first political FHQ. This is a previously unpublished photo. *HHA*

The address Tal #s 54–55 was the location of the Sterneckerbräu beer hall, "the birthplace of the Nazi Party." *The address is now Tal #38. HHA*

A good view of its main meeting room, 1933. *HHA*

(Above) Hitler's "small, vaulted room" in the Sterneckerbräu was the Party's first headquarters, complete with the initial Nazi flag over the window and a typewriter in the foreground, and the Führer's first office. *HHA*

(Above) The opposite end of the same room, with portraits of (from left to right) unknown, Dr. Josef Göbbels, Hermann Göring, Adolf Hitler, Gen. Franz Ritter (Knight) von Epp, and unknown, called the "first seven battling guards" in the legend on the wall at top right, "who laid the cornerstone of the German freedom movement." The inscription on the wall reads, "In this corner, on February 24, 1920, our Chancellor, Adolf Hitler, established the NSDAP [National Socialist German Workers' Party, or Nazi for short]. The first seven brave champions here laid the cornerstone of the German freedom movement," and that's how most Nazis saw it in 1933. *HHA*

(Right) Nazi propaganda painting titled *In the Beginning Was the Word,* by artist Hermann Otto Hoyer, depicting Army stool pigeon (and newly discovered orator) Adolf Hitler holding forth to an early audience. *U.S. Army Combat Art Collection*

(Above) American Army GIs standing outside the Hofbräuhaus in Munich. It had just become the command post of the 157th Infantry Regiment, U.S. 45th Division, as stenciled on the wall in front. *SC*

(Right) The Hofbräuhaus in 1989. *Donald Jacobs.* (Inset) The Nazi plaque in the Festival Hall of the Hofbräuhaus, commemorating the historic meeting of February 24, 1920, and the adoption of the Party's Twenty-five Point program. *The party's first mass meeting took place there on October 16, 1919. HHA*

After the Party was reestablished in 1925 (it had been legally dissolved following the failure of the Bürgerbräukeller Putsch), the Führer chaired a small executive committee meeting. Pictured from left to right are Gregor Strasser, Dr. Friedrich Weber, Adolf Hitler, Franz Xavier Schwarz, Max Amann, and Ulrich Graf. With their backs to the camera in the foreground are Karl Fiehler (left) and Julius Schaub. *HHA*

(Left) The Hofbräuhaus interior during the Third Reich, with chairs on top of tables. The chairs were used as weapons during the brawls of the 1920s, and Hitler himself narrowly missed being hit in the head by a thrown chair as well as by several beer mugs. *HHA*

(Left) At the Hofbräuhaus on February 24, 1940, during the war—and the twentieth anniversary of the Party—(center, left to right) Heinrich Himmler, Rudolf Hess, Hermann Esser, Adolf Hitler, and Julius Schaub give the Nazi salute in this previously unpublished photograph. *HHA*

(Left) The destroyed Hofbräuhaus interior in 1945. It was rebuilt after the war, minus any Nazi memorials, and is still the most famous beer hall in the world. *SC*

(Above) A recent photograph of the Löwenbräukeller beer hall at Nymphenburgerstrasse #4 in Munich. *Steven Lehrer*

(Right) On November 9, 1943, Hitler spoke from the lectern of the Löwenbräukeller (at right) as he gave the twentieth-anniversary commemoration of the Bürgerbräukeller Putsch before the Party's Old Fighters. Clapping front and center, from left to right, were Göbbels, Göring, and Martin Bormann (behind microphone stems). *HHA*

The Café Gastotte at Corneliusstrasse #12 was the second Nazi Party headquarters, after the Sterneckerbräu beer hall. *HHA*

(Above) In May 1945, British and American soldiers stood on the front steps of the main building of the Bürgerbräukeller, site of the failed November 8–9, 1923, putsch. In this picture, it has become the CP of the U.S. 157th Infantry Division. *SC*

(Above) Swastika banners and a Nazi wreath marked the exterior of Hitler's Landsberg prison cell until 1945. *HHA*

Bavarian fortress Landsberg am Lech (River) prison, where Hitler served nine months' time during 1924. *HHA*

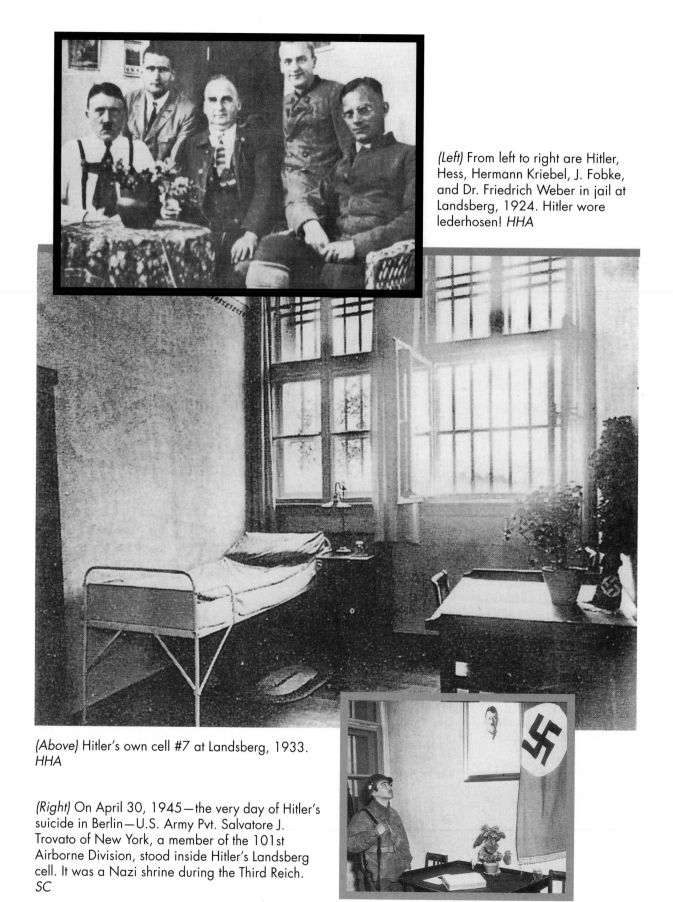

(Left) From left to right are Hitler, Hess, Hermann Kriebel, J. Fobke, and Dr. Friedrich Weber in jail at Landsberg, 1924. Hitler wore lederhosen! *HHA*

(Above) Hitler's own cell #7 at Landsberg, 1933. *HHA*

(Right) On April 30, 1945—the very day of Hitler's suicide in Berlin—U.S. Army Pvt. Salvatore J. Trovato of New York, a member of the 101st Airborne Division, stood inside Hitler's Landsberg cell. It was a Nazi shrine during the Third Reich. *SC*

(Above) On February 27, 1925, Hitler addressed the Party's top leadership for the first time since his early release from Landsberg prison in December 1924. Left to right at the head table are Philip Bouhler, Ziegler, Alfred Rosenberg, Walter Buch, Franz Xavier Schwarz, Adolf Hitler (standing), Gregor Strasser, Heinrich Himmler, Karl Fiehler, and—in front of the door at right—Julius Streicher (bald head). Note, too, the Party standards, all designed by Hitler personally. *HHA*

(Left) Schellingstrasse #50 (right) was the Party's fourth headquarters in Munich during 1925–31. Its front housed Heinrich Hoffmann's photo studio, where Hitler met Eva Braun in October 1929. *HHA*

(Left) Hitler (in hat at right) held court at a table at the outdoor Café Heck in Munich. Hermann Esser is in profile at the far left. *HHA*

(Right) Hitler's apartment at Prinzregentenplatz (Prince Regent Plaza) #16 in Munich during 1929–45. His apartment was on the second floor of this building, "above the ground level [third floor in American usage]" according to Geoffrey R. Walden, *The Third Reich in Ruins*, www.thirdreichruins.com. The building is seen here in 1968. *Steven Lehrer*

(Above) In repose inside the Führer's Munich apartment on September 30, 1938, were (from left to right) Britain's Prime Minister Neville Chamberlain, Hitler, and German Foreign Office interpreter Dr. Paul Schmidt. *HHA*

(Above) For many years, authors have incorrectly identified this photo as being Hitler's office at FHQ Berghof, while in fact it is the Führer's study at his Prince Regent Plaza apartment in Munich. *HHA*

(Right) Brown House frontage with balcony over the front door, which was flanked by two iron Nazi eagle standards. *HHA*

(Left) Hitler's balcony, on the Brown House, as seen on November 9, 1933, with the massive Nazi banner overshadowing the front door below it. Hitler (left) and Franz Xavier Schwarz (right) stood on it, at center, on the tenth anniversary of the Bürgerbräukeller Putsch. *HHA*

(Below) A variation on the same theme, but this time from their view of the crowd down below. *HHA*

(Upper left) The Brown House Senate Hall. *HHA*

(Upper right) The Brown House Party treasurer's office. *HHA*

(Above) This is where the actual work was done in the Brown House. Male and female secretaries maintained the voluminous files on millions of Nazi Party members from 1929 to 1945. The Allies found the files useful during the Nuremberg Trials of 1945–49. *HHA*

(Left) Hitler's office in the Brown House. *HHA*

(Left) The Brown House, like the Third Reich itself, in ruins in 1945 from Allied bombing raids. SC

(Below) The front and left-side view of the Hotel Kaiserhof on the Wilhelmstrasse in Berlin during 1932–33, when Hitler rented the entire second floor for himself and his growing entourage. LC

(Right) A good close-up of the hotel's façade with Hitler's suite on the second floor, just behind the building's impressive signage. From his windows, Hitler could look directly across the street at his future home, the Old Reich Chancellery. LC

(Left) Hermann and Emmy Göring's wedding procession pulled up at the entrance to the Kaiserhof on April 10, 1935, with them in the lead car. *HGA*

(Below) A good interior shot of the Hotel Kaiserhof's famous café lounge, where Chancellor Hitler held court daily during the early years of his tenure in office. *LC*

(Left) A Nazi Party caucus of Reichstag deputies at the Kaiserhof on September 6, 1932, showing (from left to right) Göring, Wilhelm Frick, Hitler (saluting and not waving), Gregor Strasser, Göbbels (rear), and Wilhelm Stoehr. *HHA*

(Above) Victory! Chancellor Hitler assembled his trusted minions at the Hotel Kaiserhof for a group photograph celebrating his appointment as head of the German government on January 30, 1933. Seen from left to right are: Erich Kube, Kurmark, Frick (seated), Göbbels, Hitler, Ernst Röhm, Göring, Dr. Walter Darre, and Himmler. Not shown in this photo but at the gathering were Otto Wagener on far left and Rudolf Hess at far right. At this time, only Hitler, Frick, and Göring were Nazi Party members of what was actually a conservative coalition cabinet designed to "contain" the radical Nazis. It failed to do so, and within eighteen months, Hitler was the complete dictator. HHA

(Right) In 1945, the Hotel Kaiserhof was a destroyed shell of its old self; amazingly, though, the front signage on the famous entranceway at far left survived both the Allied bombing raids and the Battle of Berlin. LC

The Führer's prewar air travel: (Right) Hitler's personal D-2600 Junkers Ju-52 "Auntie Ju" aircraft over the Zeppelinwiese at Nuremberg, September, 1934; (Below) The Führer deplanes from his Ju-52 in this previously-unpublished photo. *HHA*

THE OLD REICH CHANCELLERY

The *Machtegreifung*—The Nazi "Seizure of Power," January 30, 1933–August 2, 1934

The newly appointed Reich Chancellor Hitler served at the pleasure of Reich President Paul von Hindenburg and could have been dismissed from office by him until the latter's death on August 2, 1934. After von Hindenburg's death, Hitler illegally violated the German Constitution by merging both his office and that of the president into one, with his new title being Führer and Reich chancellor. Hitler thus united the Party and the state for the first time, with the latter being run by the former. Hitler also made the entire German Armed Forces take an oath of allegiance to him, personally, rather than to the constitution or state.

All non-Nazi organizations, parties, and institutions were either abolished outright or taken over by Nazi replacements, the *Gleischaltung* (coordination) having already been worked out at the various earlier FHQs during the years of the Kampfzeit. In March 1933, the German Reichstag passed the Enabling Bill that gave Chancellor Hitler domestic dictatorial powers, and these powers were not revoked until the end of the regime.

The 2005 Russian study *The Hitler Book* quotes Hitler as saying, "I have my own Party! I am the Führer! I am not a Chancellor of the old school! I am Hitler!" He was not yet, however, complete master of his realm, as the German Armed Forces still eluded his total control. The leaders had sworn a personal oath of allegiance to Hitler by name after von Hindenburg's demise, but that did not ensure his absolute dominance.

The Third Reich administrators ruled from two official government buildings in the national capital of Berlin—the Old and New Reich Chancelleries—as well as from the Führerbau (Leader Building) in Munich and Hitler's two vacation homes in Bavaria, the Berghof (Mountain Homestead) and the Kehlsteinhaus nearby. In addition to those two structures, the official government and Party chancelleries that housed the necessary administrative staffs were located at neighboring Bischofswiesen in southern Germany, the so-called Second Chancellery.

The Old Reich Chancellery in Berlin: Hitler's Governmental, Political, and Military FHQ, 1933–45

In his postwar memoir, *I Burned Hitler*, SS Col. Erich Kempka recalled that upon becoming chancellor in 1933, Hitler told him, "'Do you know, Kempka, I will not come out of this alive?' These words touched me then, and I will not forget them."

How different was the jubilant Nazi Führer on January 30, 1933, as he told photographer Heinrich Hoffmann of his appointment as Reich chancellor, which is recalled in *Hitler Was My Friend*: "All's well—the Old Gentleman (von Hindenburg) has signed it." In his diary, Dr. Göbbels was more prescient in his view of their tenure in the Berlin Chancellery: "No force on earth will get us out of here alive!"

When Hitler entered the Old Reich Chancellery (Old RC) officially, von Hindenburg warned him, "Stay to the walls [of the room], Hitler!" forecasting that he was actually expecting the floor to collapse.

As soon as he took office, Chancellor Hitler immediately ordered that the Old RC be completely structurally rebuilt and cosmetically remodeled. Next to one of the big reception rooms he added a music room and dining hall, designed by his official architect, Dr. Paul Ludwig Troost. The United Munich Workshop of Dr. Gerdy Troost, the architect's wife provided the interior design and furniture of these rooms.

Being an almost perfect square, the lofty dining hall had a trio of glass french doors that opened out onto the famed Chancellery park (referred to, wrongly, in all post–Third Reich Allied accounts as "the Reich Chancellery garden"). A great, twenty-foot-wide painting by artist F. August Kaulbach, titled *The Entry of the Sun Goddess*, was hung on one of the dining hall's walls. Two life-size bronze statues by Munich sculptor Prof. Josef Wackerle—Blood and Earth—stood in niches. The large table, when fully extended, sat sixty diners, and there were also smaller tables for the adjutants of the Führer's daily guests plus a buffet. Initially intended as only a dining hall, the room later evolved into a private site where visiting heads of state and foreign diplomats could dine officially—but also privately—with the German Reich chancellor.

Specially trained SS (Security Service) men were the liveried waiters and wore short, white jackets and black trousers. Their service was silent and discreet. The usual fare reflected Hitler's own rather simple tastes in food: soup, a course of meat (which he didn't eat) with vegetables (which he did), and a light dessert. Those who were also vegetarians, as was the Führer, had their meals prepared by a special, on-site cook. Reportedly, only Martin Bormann ever availed himself of the Führer's own strict diet.

From the very outset, the new chancellor declared that the Old RC was far too small for his needs and was to be rebuilt accordingly. Since October 1932, the residential wing at Wilhelmstrasse #77 was occupied by Field Marshal von Hindenburg himself, while his own presidential palace was being renovated; thus, Hitler was prevented from moving in.

The chancellor was initially housed in the rooms of Old RC State Secretary Dr. Otto Meissner, but he finally moved into his own quarters in the fall of 1933. Straightaway he commissioned Dr. Troost to refurbish his apartment on the building's first floor. The Führer situated his new office on the park side of the structure, adjacent to an ambassadorial reception hall, with an adjoining room for his own adjutants. The building's prior conference room was expanded and refurnished as the new Reich Cabinet Room.

Next to that were a smaller private office, living and bedrooms (the latter with adjoining bathrooms), and a terrace on the roof that was for the chancellor's private use. There were also several smaller guest rooms built facing the Wilhelmstrasse. Eva Braun used two of these starting early in 1939 during her rare visits to the capital.

According to John Toland in *Adolf Hitler*, "At night, he [Hitler] would invariably lock himself in his Spartan bedroom. . . . In the morning . . . [o]nly when he was putting on his jacket would he emerge from his room, greet [Karl] Krause [his valet] and proceed to the library for a breakfast of two cups of milk, up to 10 pieces of zwieback and several pieces of semi-sweet chocolate. He would eat erect while examining reports from [the] DNB—the German News Bureau. Breakfast was over in five minutes and, without pause, he set off for the office."

The entire ground level of the Old RC was also largely reconstructed, with a park-side annex to the salon there revamped into an impressive reception room. On the street, or the right, side of the building were a pair of living rooms, the dining hall, and the formal indoor Winter Garden, which was well liked by all. On the park, or left, side were twin movie projection rooms, plus a cloakroom and a guardroom, all designed and built by Speer.

Within his first sixteen months in office, Hitler concentrated his executive powers as chancellor (prime minister); head of state (akin to the president of the United States); nominal commander in chief of the Armed Forces; and Führer of the Nazi Party, a civilian, political entity. To reflect all this grandeur, the Reich chancellor requested and got a larger reception hall that could hold fully two hundred people for official functions of state, such as the annual gathering of the foreign diplomatic corps after the New Year.

Meanwhile, on the Foreign Ministry side, twin two-room and triple-room staff apartments were also added. All of these structures—according to new ordinances governing all new military and public buildings—were mandated to have bomb shelters placed underneath for expected air raids. Indeed, the Old RC shelter was personally designed by would-be architect Hitler himself, indicating that even in 1933, at the very start of his rule, he was planning for war.

Noted Hoffmann in *Hitler Was My Friend*, "Because of his experiences during the First World War, Hitler considered himself to be an expert on the construction of shelters." This trend continued until the last days of World War II.

Press Chief Dr. Otto Dietrich, in his postwar memoir, *Hitler*, added the Führer's "apartment in Berlin was at Wilhelmstrasse #71. On the first and second floors of the Old Reich Chancellery . . . he . . . promptly had Bismarck's apartment rebuilt, with no respect whatsoever for its historical associations. It was also furnished in severe classical style, with interesting color schemes by Munich interior decorators"—in other words, Dr. Gerty Troost. "Hitler himself made sketches for the new furniture," which she then duly had built for him.

The Führerstandarte

The Führer Standard—designed personally by Hitler—was a flag flown wherever he was in either official residence or attendance. However, it was not used at any of his wartime military field FHQs or his vacation homes: the Berghof, the Mosslahnerkopf Small Teahouse, or the Kehlsteinhaus. It also appeared in a larger format on the front of the Nuremberg Party Congress Hall on the Zeppelin Field Building until 1939 and in a smaller form on the front of his various Mercedes-Benz cars, complete with wartime camouflage cover.

Hitler's "Flower Wars"—The "Bloodless" Conquests of 1935–39

The 1935–39 Flower Wars were so called because they were all achieved without even a shot fired in anger, while the residents of the areas that were absorbed tossed flowers at Hitler and his German troops.

The former German Saarland voted to return home to the Reich rather than remain with the French occupying power in 1935, while Hitler marched into the formerly demilitarized German Rhineland in March 1936 and took it back. The *Anschluss* (union) with Austria followed in March 1938. The following September the Allies handed the Führer the Czech Südetenland at the Munich Pact Conference because he claimed that the German minority there was being oppressed and the Allies wished to avoid a general war.

Breaking his pledge of not making any more territorial demands in Central Europe, the Führer's forces seized the Czech capital of Prague and, with it, Bohemia and Moravia on March 15, 1939.

Next came the German occupation of the Baltic seaport of Memel on March 23, a former German territory given to Lithuania by the 1919 Treaty of Versailles. It was his invasion of Poland on September 1, 1939, however, that led to the general European war that no one—not even Hitler himself—actually wanted.

On September 3, Great Britain and France declared war on Germany. On June 10, 1940, Fascist Italy joined Hitler's side. The Führer attacked Russia on June 22, 1941. When his Tripartite Pact partner Japan launched a surprise assault against the United States the following December 7, it instantly transformed the former European war into World War II, in British Prime Minister Winston Churchill's apt phrase.

But several important events at the Old German Reich Chancellery in Berlin preceded these wartime developments.

Design for War: The Hossbach Conference at the Old RC

On June 24, 1937, Defense (later War) Minister Gen. Werner von Blomberg issued a top secret directive about possible future wartime scenarios that might involve the German Reich. To discuss these and other industrial problems facing Nazi Germany, he called a meeting at the Old RC on the afternoon of November 5, 1937.

A formerly unheard-of type of meeting, it was kept secret even from the full Reich Cabinet. It formally began at 4:15 PM, and ended four hours and fifteen minutes later, according to a man who was there and took down the minutes.

His name was Col. Friedrich Hossbach, and on August 3, 1934, he had become the Führer's personal Army adjutant. At the same time he served as the division chief in the Army Personnel Office and was responsible for all appointments within that branch of the military services. He produced what became known at the first Nuremberg Trial as the "Hossbach Memorandum."

Indeed, this fateful meeting and its resultant document would be the core of the conspiracy charges against the Nazi military at the subsequent Allied International Military Tribunal at Nuremberg during 1945–46.

Hitler excluded all other adjutants from the session, including his own five. So those present were himself, von Blomberg, Army Commander in Chief Gen. Werner von Fritsch, Navy Commander in Chief Adm. Dr. Erich Raeder, Foreign Minister Baron Konstantin von Neurath, and Luftwaffe (Air Force) head Gen. Hermann Göring, Hitler's number two man.

The chancellor stressed that Nazi Germany must achieve economic independence so that it would not be strangled by a British naval blockade as imperial Germany had been in World War I. He also focused on German population growth, stressing the need for future living space for the planned expansion of the German Reich.

Unlike the abdicated German Kaiser (Emperor) Wilhelm II—who began a German colonial empire overseas in Africa and the Pacific—Hitler instead sought this needed territory by conquest. First he looked to then-Russian lands to the east, in the Communist Union of Soviet Socialist Republics (USSR).

Speaking in a typical monologue, Hitler told his listeners that he hoped to prepare the way for his great war of conquest in the Soviet Union with a series of smaller wars with Austria, Czechoslovakia, and Poland, on the model of Prussian King Frederick the Great. He hoped to acquire them peaceably by diplomacy, but he was prepared to go to war with them and, if necessary, to wage a general European war against both Great Britain and France.

The Führer added that the major war he foresaw with Soviet dictator Josef Stalin must take place before 1943–45, when all of the then-currently produced German weaponry would become obsolete (as, indeed, it did). No one present raised any moral objections against starting a war of aggression, but Göring stated the Reich might want to end its involvement in the Spanish Civil War. Hitler, though, declined to do so at that time.

Admiral Raeder was silent. Both soldiers who were present—Field Marshal von Blomberg and Colonel-General von Fritsch—protested the Third Reich wasn't yet ready for a potential two-front war against the united Allied powers. Von Neurath concurred. Hitler seethed with rage, angry that his proposals were not being supported. The meeting ended, and within six months both soldiers had been forced to resign. Von Neurath was replaced by Joachim von Ribbentrop, Göring was made a Luftwaffe field marshal, and Hitler himself—à la Mussolini—took over the war minister's post with the creation of the Oberkommando des Wehrmacht (OKW, or the Armed Forces High Command).

Hitler's Old Reich Chancellery Coup Against His Military, February 4–6, 1938

On March 16, 1935, the old Reichswehr (Reich Armed Forces, 1919–35) was transformed into the new Wehrmacht (literally, Military Power, or Armed Forces, 1935–45), and Minister of Defense von Blomberg's title was also changed to minister of war.

On Hitler's forty-seventh birthday—April 20, 1936—the Führer appointed him the first field marshal of the new Third Reich. He had toyed with the idea of naming him to the novel post of Reich marshal instead, but he reserved that new title for Göring in 1940. Additionally, Gen. Erich Ludendorff—the famed quartermaster general of World War I—had spurned Hitler's offer of the same field marshalship before.

On February 4, 1938, the Führer conducted a purge of his conservative Old Guard by firing the reactionary Foreign Minister von Neurath and his two top soldiers—the field marshal and his Army Commander in Chief von Fritsch. He promoted Göring instead as the first of his Luftwaffe field marshals, thus making him the ranking military man in Nazi Germany, a position that he held until almost the end of the war in 1945.

The Reich chancellor formally announced all of these changes on February 6, 1938, in a document that began thus: "As of now, I am personally assuming direct command of the entire Wehrmacht. The former Department of the Wehrmacht in the Reich Ministry of War—with all its assignments—comes directly under my command as the High Command of the Wehrmacht and as my military staff.

"The former Chief of the Department of the Wehrmacht [Gen. Wilhelm Keitel] becomes Chief of Staff of OKW with the title 'Chief of the OKW.' His rank is equivalent to that of a Reich Minister." Keitel reported to Hitler directly.

In one fell swoop, Chancellor Hitler toppled the major military check on his overall power since 1933: he took on the posts of minister of war and the Army commander in chief on December 19, 1941, after firing von Fritsch's successor, Field Marshal Walther von Brauchitsch.

Hitler's Work Habits

According to Nikolaus von Below, Hitler's Luftwaffe adjutant during 1937–45, in his postwar memoir *At Hitler's Side,* "With the exception of the most urgent business, during the day he never used a desk except to sit on it. It was his rather odd custom to burst into a sudden dictation, and his adjutants would have to scribble down instructions and intentions and later practically recast them. These would be sudden inspirations and incomplete ideas. Errors in taking down the notes could have serious consequences."

Von Below added, "During the afternoon, he would retire to his private rooms to read or rest, although in good weather he enjoyed a walk in the Reich Chancellery park." During the war, however, Hitler transformed himself as much as he could into a workaholic, displaying a discipline that he'd never shown before—something that few of his many biographers have accurately reported.

The Plunge Toward War

By the time of the September 1938 Czech Südetenland crisis, Hitler was sure of his hold over the German people and their support of his future war plans, but in this he erred. On the morning of September 27, 1938, newspapers announced that a parade of the Army's crack Second Motorized Division would pass by the Old RC on its way, presumably, to the coming war with the Czechs.

Hitler believed that this would incite the kind of popular demonstrations for the war that he'd been part of in Munich in August 1914, but he was wrong. The people in the street sullenly watched the troops march by without any cheering, singing, or fervid Nazi salutes. American radio announcer William L. Shirer, who was there, stated that the irate Führer sulkily stalked off his famed balcony, back inside the Old RC, and let his men pass by unreviewed.

On September 3, 1939, everyone expected that Hitler would remain in the Old RC–New RC complex and direct the Polish campaign from there, but they were shocked when he went to the front in person aboard his special train, code-named *Amerika.* It was aboard special train *Brandenburg* (the code-name was changed on February 1, 1943) that Hitler returned to Berlin for the final time from the Western Front after the failed Battle of the Bulge. According to his SS valet, Heinz Linge, in his memoir *Until the Fall,* at 9:40 AM on January 16, 1945, Hitler entered the Old RC once more.

In the Old Reich Chancellery for the Last Time, 1945

By then, Allied air raids had demolished the Cabinet Room, the music hall, the smoking room, and the Winter Garden, all built in 1936; however, his own apartment and the rest of the second floor remained as yet undamaged. All the windows had been blown out, though, and fallen plaster littered the floor. After some repairs, however, all the rooms were made usable again, and Hitler lived once more in his former apartment.

His second-floor, park-side office had also been hit, but it was repaired and he continued to work there until mid-March 1945. Hoffmann recalled, "This room was also used for the daily military briefings. Hitler continued to sleep in his bedroom on the second floor until he moved into the bunker because of the daily [mostly nightly] air raids."

The exact date on which the Führer descended into the famous bunker is in doubt. Both SS Gen. Julius Schaub and Hitler's secretary, Johanna Wolf, claimed that he slept upstairs until February 27–28, 1945, while another secretary—Christa Schröder—stated that he went below for good in the first days in March because of the constant enemy air raids that enervated him.

By that time, the famed Reich Chancellery park had been heavily damaged by enemy bombs. Its lawns were potted with craters, its trees were broken and torn by shrapnel, and the formerly carefully tended walking paths were no longer distinguishable.

(Left) A panoramic view of the Old Reich Chancellery complex as seen from across the Wilhelmstrasse on the Hotel Kaiserhof's side of the street. The eighteenth-century original Prussian structure (right) had an annex built (left) in the late 1920s, and during 1938–39, Speer built Hitler's New RC to the south of the annex. *HHA*

(Right) The same eighteenth-century Prussian Old RC in ruins after the war, in 1946. *LC*

(Bottom right) A good close-up of the 1920s annex of the original Old RC, as seen in 1935. It was Chancellor Hitler's official seat of government power and his residence. Speer built him the famous balcony on the second floor in the middle of the main building, from which he saluted passing troops on parade and pro-Nazi crowds. His office on this side of the building was very noisy because it faced the street. It quickly became stuffy if the windows were shut, so he moved his working office to a different room at the rear of the building that faced the park—where he would be cremated and buried in 1945. *HHA*

In front of the Old Reich Chancellery's original eighteenth-century Prussian courtyard, the Führer stands in his Mercedes-Benz 770K Grosser parade car to salute the Leibstandarte (Lifeguard) SS Adolf Hitler Regiment stomping down the Wilhelmstrasse on his fiftieth birthday, April 20, 1939. Heinrich Himmler (left) and Sepp Dietrich (right) stand in front of the car. *HHA*

(Right) The inner courtyard of the Old Reich Chancellery in 1936. *HHA*

(Left) The rear façade of the Old Chancellery, facing the park. Hitler was sworn in as chancellor in the room behind the three windows on the left side of the second floor. *LC*

(Right) Hitler, followed by Wilhelm Frick, gives an informal Nazi salute on the day of Hitler's appointment as chancellor, January 30, 1933. An SS guard, Otto Gesche, follows them. Note also the pair of German Army sentries. *HHA*

(Right) In this photo, President von Hindenburg's grandchildren are seen at a fountain at the rear of the Old Reich Chancellery. As can be seen plainly here, the "garden" behind the entire Reich Chancellery complex was actually a sizable park. *LC*

(Right) In the first official photograph of Hitler as Reich chancellor, he is seen at his desk in the Old Reich Chancellery on January 30, 1933. *HHA*

(Far right) A tuxedo-clad Hitler listens to election returns on March 5, 1933, in the Old RC on either a Telefunken or Loewa Opta radio (left, on the table) and speaker box set at right. *HHA*

(Above) On February 1, 1933, the new chancellor made his first national radio broadcast from the Old RC. *HHA*

(*Left*) Hitler makes his nightly telephone call from the Old RC to Eva Braun in the Berghof at Obersalzberg. In 2005, the editors of the Russian-produced work *The Hitler Book* revealed this amusing anecdote about the RC phone service: "There were often crossed lines, which led to absurd situations. When someone asked him [Hitler] who he was—and he told them the truth—the voice at the other end replied, 'You must be really crazy!' In Bayreuth, someone called him to ask the time. Then on another occasion when he was speaking to Eva Braun, someone broke in to say, 'Private conversations are not allowed here.'" *HHA*

In this previously unpublished photograph, Hitler gives his informal Nazi salute from atop his famous balcony at the Old RC annex. On the night of January 30, 1933, Dr. Josef Göbbels organized a torchlight parade of Nazi Party formations to march past the Old RC in honor of Hitler's appointment as Reich chancellor. Since no balcony yet existed, Hitler, Hess, and Göring leaned out of a window to salute the marchers, and because all of them couldn't fit in it comfortably at the same time, the annoyed Führer ordered Speer to build the structure seen here, with french doors opening out onto the Wilhelmstrasse façade. *HHA*

(Right) In this previously unpublished shot, we see an excellent interior view of the Old RC, most likely after the first Hitler-Speer remodeling of 1933–34. *HHA*

(Far right) This photo shows Hitler's predominantly conservative (non-Nazi) first cabinet of 1933, which was intended to control him—it didn't. From left to right are: Minister of Labor Dr. Franz Seldte, Justice Minister Dr. Franz Gurtner, Minister of Propaganda and Public Enlightenment Dr. Göbbels, Minister of Posts Paul Baron von Eltz-Rubenach, Hitler, Prime Minister of Prussia and Minister of Aviation Göring, unknown man, Defense Minister General von Blomberg, Minister of the Interior Frick, Foreign Minister von Neurath, Reichsbank President Dr. Hjalmar Schacht, Finance Minister Baron Lutz Schwerin von Krosigk, unknown official, and Vice Chancellor Franz von Papen in Hitler's Old RC office. (Missing is Alfred Hugenberg, Minister for Economics and Food). *HHA*

(Left) Hitler troops the line of an Army honor guard in the Reich Presidential Palace's inner courtyard after a diplomatic reception in 1933. *HHA*

On New Year's Day, 1934, and each year thereafter through 1939, the chancellor and his cabinet received the Foreign Diplomatic Corps. From left to right are: von Papen, von Blomberg, Göring, unknown aide, Dr. Göbbels, von Krosigk, SA general Wilhelm Bruckner, Rudolf Hess, Dr. Gurtner, SA Staff Chief Capt. Ernst Röhm (obscured), Hitler (reading von Hindenburg's presidential welcome address), Dr. Walther Darre, Dr. Hans Heinrich Lammers, Dr. Schacht, and three unidentified men at the far right. Hitler sincerely venerated the Reich president as a father figure—and his constitutional superior, who could dismiss him from office at any time. *HHA*

The Reich Cabinet in session (March 17, 1935) at the announcement of the National Defense Law that reinstituted the military draft for men and created a new, stronger German Armed Forces in violation of the Versailles Peace Treaty. In the cabinet room of the Old RC are, from left to right: Dr. Hans Frank, Dr. Göbbels, presidential state secretary Dr. Hans Meissner, Frick, Prussian Finance Minister Dr. Johannes Popitz, Education Minister Dr. Bernhard Rust, Göring in the newly introduced blue Luftwaffe uniform, Fritz Sauckel, von Neurath, Hitler, Dr. Lammers, von Blomberg, Dr. Schacht, Dr. Gurtner, von Krosigk, Darre, von Eltz-Rubenach, Dr. Seldte, and Walther Funk. The Führer had just taken his first bold step toward public rearmament and, later, war. *HHA*

(Above left) In the Old RC on March 30, 1935, discussing the new Anglo-German Naval Agreement, from left to right, are: unknown aide, British officials Anthony Eden and Sir John Simon, Hitler, German Foreign Office interpreter Dr. Paul Schmidt, von Neurath, British Ambassador to Germany Sir Eric Phipps, and von Ribbentrop. According to Stefan Lorant in *Sieg Heil!* "Hitler proposed a German fleet whose [*sic*] total tonnage would be only 35% that of the British fleet—thus British superiority would be maintained." The British concurred, but the deal gave Nazi Germany a new battle fleet for virtually nothing in return. *HHA*

(Above right) In a previously unpublished photograph, the Nazi chieftains hold forth in a relaxed manner in the Old RC Cabinet Room. From left to right are: Dr. Göbbels, Göring, von Neurath, Frank, Dr. Meissner, Dr. Rust, Funk, Dr. Seldte, and Dr. Lammers. *HHA*

This previously unpublished photograph on March 17, 1935, shows a light moment before the solemn public ceremonies in Berlin's Old RC marking the rebirth of the German Armed Forces on Heroes' Memorial Day, which honored the German dead of World War I. From left to right are: Göring, Hitler, von Blomberg, German Field Marshal August von Mackensen, Adm. Dr. Erich Raeder, and Col. Gen. Wernher von Fritsch. Hitler laughed at Göring's remark just as the shutter clicked. *HHA*

(Right) Hitler's refur-
bished office in the Old
Reich Chancellery,
1934. This office,
designed by architect
Dr. Troost, faced the
park and was extremely
modest by the Führer's
later standards. *HHA*

In this previously unpublished photo, the tuxedo-clad chancellor (left) is in conversation with Gen. Hiroshi
Oshima, the Japanese military attaché, at his country's embassy in Berlin. Oshima later became the
ambassador. Note their reflection in the Old RC mirror. *JRA*

(Right) This is a previously unpublished photograph of Hitler's forty-seventh birthday celebration in the Old RC on April 20, 1936. From left to right are: Admiral Dr. Raeder, von Blomberg (appointed the first field marshal of the Third Reich, seen here with his new baton), Hitler, Göring as commander in chief of the Luftwaffe, and Gen. Gerd von Rundstedt, standing in for the absent von Fritsch. *HGA*

(Above) On March 2, 1938, inside the Old RC. From left to right are: former President of the United States Herbert Hoover, Hitler, Dr. Schmidt, and U.S. Ambassador to Germany Hugh Wilson. It was a grim session for all concerned, as the Führer confronted the only American president he would ever meet face to face. During the heated meeting—according to Herbert Norton Smith's *An Uncommon Man: The Triumph of Herbert Hoover*—"Hitler leapt to his feet and ranted for several minutes without interruption, until Hoover . . . told him to sit down. 'That's enough . . . I'm not interested in your views.'" *Herbert Hoover Library, West Branch, Iowa*

(Left) The Führer-standarte, Hitler's flag or banner with his personal insignia. (Above) The large, 20-by-20-foot banner that was hung at the Zeppelin Field at Nuremberg during the annual Party rally. *HHA*

(Above) In August 1939 in the Old RC, an ecstatic Führer (left) welcomes home from Moscow von Ribbentrop, the man he called his "Second Bismarck," after he signed the Nazi-Soviet Non-Aggression Pact with Stalin. From left to right are: Hitler; Foreign Office Ambassador Walther Hewel; Army adjutant Gerhard Engel; Göring's liaison officer to Hitler, Gen. Karl Bodenschatz (wearing civilian suit); Foreign Office aide Dr. Reinhard Spitzy (today a frequent History Channel guest); von Ribbentrop; Foreign Office state secretary Ernst von Weizacker; Nazi Motor Corps Führer aide Albert Bormann (younger brother of Martin Bormann); and SS aide to Hitler, Max Wunsche. *HHA*

(Above) In April 1941, Reich Marshal Göring (center) and Hitler (right) welcome Japanese Foreign Minister Yosuke Matsuoka to the Old RC, with Dr. Schmidt (second from left) serving as the interpreter. In the background is the famous portrait of Frederick the Great by Anton Graf that the Führer gave his personal pilot, Hans Baur, as a parting gift just before Hitler's suicide on April 30, 1945. *HHA*

(Left) This is a photograph of the June 14, 1941, Old RC military conference in Berlin that preceded the invasion of the Soviet Union by just eight days. Assembled were all the service chiefs and Army group commanders, plus those of armies and panzer (armored) groups. At this conference the Führer explained the final details of Operation Barbarossa. From left to right are: Luftwaffe Gen. Erhard Milch, two unknown officers, von Brauchitsch (and behind him four unidentified men), then–Army Gen. Walther von Reichenau, the Austrian-born Luftwaffe Gen. Alexander Löhr, Luftwaffe Chief of General Staff Col. Hans Jeschonneck, Army General Ritter, von Schobert, Hitler, and Keitel. *HHA*

3 FHQ BERGHOF, MOOSLAHNERKOPF TEAHOUSE, BISCHOFSWIESEN CHANCELLERY, AND KEHLSTEINHAUS

The young Hitler relocated his personal headquarters to Haus Wachenfeld on the Oberzalzberg (Mountain Over the Salt Mine) near the town of Berchtesgaden in 1925, following his release from Landsberg Fortress. Initially, he rented Haus Wachenfeld, but in June 1933, using his book royalties from the success of *Mein Kampf*, he was able to purchase the small cottage outright for 40,000 Goldmarks.

Reichsleiter (National Leader) Martin Bormann, Nazi Deputy Führer Rudolf Hess's representative, began buying up vast tracts of land on the mountain in Hitler's name. The area was eventually called "Hitler Territory." Starting in 1935, the new Berghof was literally built up around the existing shell of the old Haus Wachenfeld and was completed in its final form in 1936 by architect Alois Degano.

Both before and during World War II, there were many important political, military, and diplomatic meetings, events, and conferences at this most famous private residence of a modern head of state. On February 12, 1938, Reich Chancellor Hitler—with a trio of German generals in tow—met in his second-floor office with his fellow Austrian counterpart, Federal Chancellor Kurt von Schuschnigg, to make political demands of their common native land. When the latter balked and, once back home, tried to evade compliance with Nazi demands, Hitler decided on a peaceful invasion of Austria and simply drove across the frontier in a motorized column. The majority of the Austrian people welcomed the German incursion, and at length Hitler annexed Austria outright to Germany to form the newly proclaimed Greater German Reich, or empire.

At the Berghof during his talks with the Austrian chancellor, Hitler employed a famous bit of play-acting to frighten his guest by bellowing out, "Keitel!" According to Keitel's postwar memoir, *In the Service of the Reich*: "I entered Hitler's study just as Schuschnigg was leaving it, and when I asked Hitler what commands he had for me he replied, 'None at all! Just sit down.'"

That was the only night that the future field marshal spent there in his seven-year association with Hitler. He was, however, present again the following September, when the Führer made a point of introducing him to Chamberlain so as to intimidate the British prime minister as well.

On September 3, 1938, the Führer met with Keitel and von Brauchitsch to discuss Case Green, the outright German invasion of Czechoslovakia that Hitler was determined to undertake, world war or no. Twelve days later, the Führer met with Prime Minister Chamberlain at the Berghof to demand that Great Britain and France let him have the Südetenland forthwith—or else he would take it by force and invade the Czech state.

Threatening to go home, Chamberlain thus induced the Führer to calm down. They agreed to meet a third time after the prime minister had consulted with his cabinet in London.

Later, when Hitler's speeches and demands became even more strident, it looked as if a general European war might break out at any moment. Mussolini then suggested a four-power summit to settle the whole question peaceably. Paris, Berlin, and London accepted his offer to mediate, and the infamous Munich Pact Conference was born, hosted by Hitler at the Führerbau.

The three former victors of World War I—Great Britain, Fascist Italy, and republican France—gave Hitler the Südetenland, which he promptly occupied on October 1, 1938, asserting, falsely, "We want no Czechs." On January 5, 1939, the chancellor met at the Berghof with Polish Foreign Minister Col. Josef Beck to demand certain German rights in the Polish corridor that divided German East and West Prussia and also in the free city of Danzig (today's Gdansk, Poland).

In the midst of that gathering storm—on March 15, 1939—Hitler hosted Czech President Dr. Emil Hácha at the New Reich Chancellery in Berlin and induced him, with threats of aerial bombardment of Prague and ground invasion, to "invite" German troops in to set up a formal Nazi protectorate of Prague, Bohemia, and Moravia, a

Nazi state that existed until May 1945. So it was that the Third Reich got all the Czechs as well.

In May 1939, the Führer addressed an audience of top military service chiefs and subordinate commanders at the future wartime FHQ Berghof to prepare them for the coming war with Poland but not one with the Western powers. On May 22, the Nazis and Fascists signed a military alliance called the Italian-German Pact of Steel that formally linked the Third Reich with the Duce's Italy to hopefully impress the Allies enough that they wouldn't fight for faraway Poland. It didn't work. The West stated firmly that if Germany invaded Poland, there would be war.

On August 12, the Führer received Italian Foreign Minister Count Galeazzo Ciano at the Berghof to ensure that Italy honored its recently signed treaty commitment and came into any future war at Hitler's side as a full ally. When Count Ciano returned to Rome, Hitler and Speer stood on the Berghof terrace under a blood-red sky—as Speer later recalled in *Inside the Third Reich*—leading the Führer to state, "There will be a great deal of blood. This time we won't bring it off without violence."

On August 23, Stalin sent a telegram to Hitler at the Berghof, inviting von Ribbentrop to Moscow to sign a German-Soviet Non-Aggression Pact. Thus, Hitler would not have to worry about fighting the Red Army to his rear in the east if he invaded Poland and—as a result—also had to fight Britain and France in the west. Although the pact stunned the world, the Allies remained firm in their support of Poland should the Third Reich attack.

On August 22, 1939, the Führer again addressed his assembled commanders at the Berghof on the coming war with Poland, believing he had neutralized the West, but he hadn't. He invaded Poland on September 1, and both Britain and France declared war against Berlin on the third. By September 27, the Nazis had overrun Poland, and Hitler entered the surrendered capital of Warsaw in triumph, while the Allies did nothing.

While a "phony war" ensued across the silent Western Front, Hitler took Denmark and Norway in April 1940 to ensure that his supply of iron ore continued flowing from neutral Sweden. Then he launched his all-out invasion of France and the Low Countries. The Germans defeated all enemy forces and drove the British into the sea at Dunkirk. Paris was declared an open city, the French sued for an armistice, and the war ended on June 25, 1940—but not for the British, who fought on.

Preparations to invade England—Operation Seelowe (Sea Lion)—foundered on the Luftwaffe's failure to destroy the Royal Air Force, either in the air or on the ground. Thus, on July 31, 1940—even before Göring's main aerial assault on Great Britain—Hitler called a military conference at the Berghof to discuss the invasion of his next enemy, the USSR.

On August 10, 1940, Hitler told both Keitel and Jodl that he had, indeed, decided to attack the Soviet Union (then still Germany's nominal ally) in the next year. During a two-day meeting at the Berghof on January 8–9, 1941, Hitler addressed his assembled commanders about his intention to invade the USSR. Von Below, who was there, recalled, "Not a word of opposition was raised to any of it. Their faces had a set expression. Only after leaving were the first serious questions asked."

Operation Sea Lion was postponed to begin in May 1941, but on May 10, Hitler was told that Hess had flown to Scotland to make peace between Great Britain and the Third Reich and to possibly enact a military alliance against the Soviets as well. Hess failed. Meanwhile, the Germans sent an expeditionary Afrika Korps under Gen. Erwin Rommel to North Africa to help the hapless Duce defeat the British Eighth Army, and German airborne troops took the Greek island of Crete as well.

In another move to help the Italians, the Germans invaded both mainland Greece and Yugoslavia when Yugoslavia's people rejected their alliance with Belgrade. All of this delayed Hitler's planned assault on the USSR, which finally began—five weeks late—on June 22, 1941. The quick victory over the Red Army that Hitler expected never occurred, and a planned four-month-long campaign turned into a four-year-long slugfest.

It was also at the Berghof where Gen. Franz Halder's successor as chief of the German General Staff—Gen. Kurt Zeitzler—called the Führer on November 19, 1942, to report on the Red Army counterattack that was the beginning of the end for the doomed German Sixth Army at Stalingrad. Hitler left the Obersalzberg for FHQ Wolfsschanze on the twenty-third to start dealing with an entirely new situation for him—utter defeat. Stalingrad, the German defeat in Tunisia, and Kursk turned the tide irreversibly against the Axis in 1943.

On March 19, 1944, the Führer convened a little-heralded meeting of all German field marshals at the Berghof. It included Gerd von Rundstedt, Erich von Manstein, Ewald von Kleist, Ernst Busch, Erwin Rommel, and Maximilian von Weichs.

On the way there, the marshals asked von Rundstedt to be their joint spokesman and prevail upon Hitler to give up his command of the Eastern Front and to name one of them as commander in chief or chief of staff. Von Rundstedt declined, asserting that Hitler would never agree, and he was right. Again, Hitler recalled the situation of Kaiser Wilhelm II's relationship to von Hindenburg, who deserted him with the Army High Command when the revolution at home broke out in 1918.

The cagey Hitler had anticipated just such a possible "Field Marshals' Revolt." He made them all stand in line in the Great Hall of the Berghof and read an oath of allegiance not to Germany, but to him personally. As they left him in the antechamber, Hitler stood—flanked by two SS men—with a silver tray holding rich cigars that the marshals took as they departed for their posts, less than ninety days before D-Day in Normandy.

Eleven days later, the Führer summoned von Manstein and von Kleist to the Berghof, this time to fire them personally and replace them with Gens. Walter Model and Ferdinand Schörner, respectively. Hitler told von Manstein he was being relieved because Germany's days of large-scale offensive operations in the east were over, and from then on only defensive experts such as Model and Schörner would be needed. Hitler assured him that if the Reich was ever able to return to grand blitzkrieg assaults, he would recall him to serve the flag in the field, but it never happened.

Added von Manstein aide Alexander von Stahlberg in his 1990 work *Bounden Duty*, "The man who had not even made sergeant between 1914 and 1918 had the audacity to make that outrageous remark face to face with the most important strategist of the war. . . . No one knew better than he [Hitler] that his war was long since lost." Von Manstein's response as to why he didn't lead the marshals against their Führer was simply, "Prussian Marshals do not mutiny."

Twenty days after D-Day, Hitler made his final public speaking appearance of the war at the Hotel Platterhof on the Obersalzberg to address German industrialists. Three days later, the Führer held his final conference on the Normandy crisis with Marshals Rommel and von Rundstedt at FHQ Berghof, having met with them already on June 17 at FHQ Wolfsschlucht at Margival, France.

On July 14, 1944, Hitler left FHQ Berghof for the last time and returned to Rastenburg, East Prussia. He would leave there, finally, on November 20 for Berlin, and then go on to the new Western Front to direct the Battle of the Bulge.

The Berghof's possible future career as an FHQ site ended for good with the RAF bomber attack of Wednesday, April 25, 1945. Martin Bormann still urged Hitler to return to the surviving air-raid tunnels of the Alpine redoubt—a scenario that was feared by the Americans—to play for negotiating time or, if necessary, to make a final stand on the Obersalzberg, but Hitler remained adamant: he would die in his capital, Berlin.

The Teahouse on the Mooslahnerkopf, Obersalzberg

Almost daily when he was in residence at the Berghof during 1937–44, the Führer led his entourage on a relaxing half-hour walk from the main house to the small teahouse on the Mooslahnerkopf, at a scenic overlook with the Bavarian Alps as a backdrop, built in 1937.

This walk was a set-piece aspect of Hitler's regimen both before and during the war. The small circular teahouse is not to be confused with the later and larger Kehlsteinhaus of 1939–45. Speer described the teahouse in his *Inside the Third Reich* as "a round room about 25′ in diameter with a row of small-paned windows and a fireplace along the interior wall."

The Führer's post-lunchtime walks ended here, with chatting over drinks and snacks. Often he napped here, too, as the conversations took on a quieter, muted tone. Hitler sometimes discussed policies with his aides as well. The guests returned by waiting cars to the Berghof at 7:00 PM. The U.S. Army blew up the teahouse and its foundation in 1951; only ruins still remained as of 2006.

Bischofswiesen, Bavaria: The Second Reich Chancellery

By 1935, Hitler was increasingly running the government from his own vacation home, the Berghof. On February 21, 1936, the Führer commissioned its architect—Degano—to design and build a Second Reich Chancellery at the small alpine town of Bischofswiesen, less than five kilometers away from Berchtesgaden, to house the necessary administrative staff. It was finished by mid-1938.

According to authors Ray and Josephine Cowdery in an e-mail to the author, "It is a bit further from the Berghof, as that was four kilometers outside of Berchtesgaden."

Steven Lehrer, in his work *Hitler Sites*, noted, "The interior conformed slavishly to Hitler's taste: hallways with columns, swastika emblems in the floors, walls paneled in dark wood, kitschy landscape paintings with toiling farmers, and a Franz von Lenbach bust of Bismarck." Added the Cowderys, "Dr. [Hans Heinrich] Lammers was in charge of the Reichskanzlei [which was a State and not a Party agency] in Bischofswiesen," where people like Speer and Keitel often visited. When the U.S. Army took the Obersalzberg in May 1945, Gen. Omar Bradley rode to Bischofswiesen in one of Hitler's own cars to be received by an honor guard; then it was turned into a U.S. Army office building. In 2002, Hitler's workroom conference table and a telephone installation remained from the Nazi era.

After a 2005 visit, the Cowderys said, "The buildings are still there, but have been redeveloped as public housing. When we inquired at the local tourist office, they told us we did not want to go there. We did, and found it is now in the center of a large development of houses."

The Kehlsteinhaus

The Kehlstein House sits atop the 6,017-foot-high Kehlstein Mountain above the Berghof. It was designed by architect Roderich Fick and financed by Martin Bormann as a fiftieth birthday present for Hitler in 1939. In *Hitler Sites*, Lehrer stated, "The large meeting rooms . . . indicate that the building was intended as a conference center rather than another modern teahouse," and the Führer did meet there with diplomats and others during 1939–40.

From the parking lot down below, bronze doors opened onto a 136-yard-long tunnel that led to the 400-foot-high elevator shaft for a 45-second ride up in a glistening car with Venetian mirrors and plush green leather seats. Working day and night for thirteen months, three thousand workers finished the $150 million project on time.

The entire peak upon which the structure sat was surrounded by a six-foot-high fence, and it was patrolled by guards. There were also hidden, remote-controlled gas capsules installed for extra protection from possible attackers or other intruders, but these were never used so far as is known.

The structure boasts five picture windows and a red marble fireplace. In *Hitler Sites* Lehrer noted,

Inside the house, a modest, pine-paneled tearoom was called the Scharitzkehl or Eva Braun Room. SS guards had a small duty room across from the kitchen. There was a study, a hallway with 24 bronze hat and coat hooks, and a cellar with supply and machinery rooms.

A terrace and colonnade on the south side of the building were later enclosed with glass. A long conference room was originally furnished with an oak table and 26 chairs.

German author Florian M. Beierl in *History of the Eagle's Nest*, observed the Eva Braun Room "was paneled with rare cembra pine wood. The two windows could be lowered and offered a marvelous panoramic view...."

The Führer had a study there as well, but reportedly he never used it for that purpose. Neither was the dining room ever used for a military conference.

In all, Hitler only made thirteen or fourteen known visits to the Kehlstein House, all during 1939–40. The reason was that he never fully trusted the elevator system, fearing that he might get stuck for good inside its shaft. Göbbels, Bormann, and von Ribbentrop all visited there but never Göring, who was Martin Bormann's mortal enemy.

The Kehlsteinhaus was not hit during the RAF bombing raid of April 25, 1945, and was captured intact by the U.S. Army. All the original furniture was looted in 1945, except for a heavy, large buffet in the dining room. In the decades since, the Kehlsteinhaus has often been used as a locale for shooting documentaries and dramatizations of the Third Reich. Today, the building is a popular tourist restaurant from May through October, when the spectacular four-mile-long road is open for tour buses only.

(Left) This superior aerial view is of the entire Berghof (Mountain Homestead) complex on the Obersalzberg, with Hitler's home at center, Martin Bormann's at upper left, the SS barracks and Hotel Platterhof above that, the SS gatehouse with sentries at lower right (center), and Hitler's walking path to the left. Hitler later said that he made most of his important political and military decisions while at the Berghof. When the Führer's black column of automobiles arrived, the Berghof's private function ceased, and it became at once the central seat of the government of the Third Reich. *HHA*

(Below) SS guard post on access road to Berghof at top right. *HHA.*

(Above) Hitler (right) welcomes Reichsführer (RFSS) Himmler to the Berghof before the war. Himmler became the head of the Nazi police state (Gestapo) and also architect of the Holocaust against the Jews, Gypsies, and others. In 1945 the RFSS was briefly the commander of Army Group Vistula in the east, barring the way of the Red Army in its drive toward Berlin. *HHA*

(Right) An SS gate sentry of Hitler's Bodyguard Regiment and Kuvasz guard dog in 1934 at the foot of Haus Wachenfeld (1916–36), the forerunner of the future Berghof (1936–45) on the Obersalzberg. Ladies were excluded from official state banquets at FHQ Berghof during the war. By the end of the war, Martin Bormann had successfully isolated Hitler from many people whom he did not wish the Führer to see. Note the two-car garage at right, the last vestige of which was destroyed by the State of Bavaria in 1996. *HHA*

(Left) A good frontal view of the completed FHQ Berghof in its final state. In the valley below, the Bavarian town of Berchtesgaden still exists just southeast of the village of Bischofswiesen, the location of the Second RC. At the top of the driveway (right) are stone steps, up which climbed kings, dictators, prime ministers, field marshals, and generals—before, during, and even after the war. *HHA*

An outstanding scenic view, looking down the steps from the top landing. Today, only the lower right portion, plus its retaining wall, is still visible. From left to right are: (center) King Carol of Romania, von Ribbentrop, Meissner, and Hitler during a prewar conference. Behind them all—across the far meadow at the tree line—is the path Hitler took for his daily half-hour walk after lunch to the teahouse on the Mooslahnerkopf. *HHA*

(Above) On October 23, 1937, seen descending the steps after a visit are, from left to right, in the foreground: Dr. Schmidt, the Duchess and Duke of Windsor (formerly British King Edward VII), Dr. Robert Ley, and Hitler. In 1940, von Ribbentrop unsuccessfully tried to kidnap the royals from neutral Spain in a possible plot to restore the duke to the British throne. Former British Prime Minister David Lloyd George also visited the Berghof on September 8, 1938. *HHA*

(Right) Chancellor Hitler (with his back to the camera) greets British Prime Minister Neville Chamberlain at 4:00 PM on September 15, 1938, on the Berghof's famous stone steps above the driveway. The others (from left to right) are: Dr. Schmidt, Albert Bormann, and Rudolf Schmundt, on the way to the Führer's office for the next of three summit meetings during the Czech crisis that almost led to war. *HHA*

(Above) An honor guard of the Leibstandarte (Lifeguard) SS Adolf Hitler Regiment (right) presents arms to salute the arrival of Japanese Ambassador Gen. Hiroshi Oshima, who salutes at left. With him (left to right) are: Schaub, Schmundt, von Ribbentrop, and an unknown aide, 1941. Imperial Japan was Nazi Germany's Far Eastern ally during the war. *JRA*

(Left) From left to right are: Mussolini, Schaub, Hitler, an unknown Italian official, Albert Bormann, Schmundt, and Keitel in April 1942. The steps were destroyed completely when the free state of Bavaria blew them up on April 20, 1952, on what would have been Hitler's sixty-third birthday. The Berghof was hit at least twice during the RAF air raid of April 25, 1945. *HHA*

(Above) These are the very same steps but seen in the spring of 1945 and under new management—that of the U.S. Army—which occupied the area until spring 1952. Note the blackened hulk of the Berghof at right, burned by retreating SS troops in advance of the American GIs's arrival. In her book *Until the Final Hour*, Traudl Junge described the wartime scene: "Sometimes the Winter Garden room was jammed with orderlies carrying maps and briefcases, looking out of place among the flowers. . . . In the spring of 1944, Hitler assembled the army commanders, staff officers and the leaders of all divisions of troops at the Hotel Platterhof and made inspiring speeches to them." *SC*

(Left) Pictured here in July 1943 from left to right are: Engel, Schmundt, and Adm. Karl-Jesco von Puttkamer. Adjutants Schmundt and Luftwaffe Colonel von Below were responsible for choosing and building all of Hitler's wartime FHQ sites and structures with the Organization Todt. *USNA*

(Right) A good wide-angle, wartime view of the Berghof terrace after a rainfall, with Hitler (right) listening to a diplomatic report from Germany's ambassador to neutral Turkey, von Papen (left), who later became Reich chancellor of the Weimar Republic. He failed to induce Turkey to openly side with Germany in World War II, as it had in World War I. Noted Glenn Infield in *The Secrets of the Eagle's Nest*, "One of Hitler's favorite rooms in the Berghof . . . was the map room . . . since he had a mania for maps. Drawers along the walls of the room were filled with maps of every part of the world. Over the fireplace in this room was a very large bronze map of Germany and Central Europe. He always kept the frontiers of his Third Reich up to date, and during the war he daily outlined the battle lines." The Berghof *"was built around Haus Wachenfeld on the west side of the original house,"* according to Geoff Walden. HHA

(Above) An extremely rare view of a solitary Führer walking near the car garage at FHQ Berghof during the war. The garage was the very last structure standing there until the mid-1990s, when it was destroyed by the Germans. *Frentz.*

(Left) Hitler sitting on his Berghof desk located on the first floor—second floor to the Americans. HHA

(Above) The Berghof's famous electronically lowered Grand Salon picture window on the front (north) wall, which measured 9 by 3.6 meters, with a globe at the left, marble map table at center, and seating arrangement at right. This is where Hitler conferred with Chamberlain on September 15, 1938, to avert a European war over the German Südetenland of Czechoslovakia. The communications room of the house was also important for the Führer, and there was a trio of men on duty there around the clock. Noted Glenn Infield in *The Secrets of the Eagle's Nest,* "A direct telephone line ran from the Berghof to Berlin and Munich. All Hitler's official messages were scrambled." *HHA*

(Right) In the late summer of 1936, Hitler and Göring used the Great Hall's marble map table to go over the projected Four-Year Economic Plan of 1936–40, designed to make the Third Reich self-sufficient for the then-coming war. The Führer planned for war in this room, and Göring, Bormann, and Speer all built homes on the mountain. In 1945, the Third U.S. Infantry Division captured all these buildings when it occupied Berchtesgaden and the Obersalzberg. After the war, the Americans closed up the air-raid shelter entrances, but then the Bavarian authorities re-opened them in the 1990s. *HGA*

(Left) An Axis wartime diplomatic conclave in front of the picture window with, from left to right, two unknown Spanish officials, Spanish Foreign Minister Serrano Süner, Dr. Schmidt, Hewel, Count Ciano, Hitler, and Schaub. The mountain seen through the window is the Untersberg. Just as at all his FHQs, while at FHQ Berghof, Hitler maintained his daily meeting regimen by holding two military situation conferences: the main one was held at noon, the follow-up briefing at midnight. Traudl Junge, in *Until the Final Hour*, remembered, "I could reach the adjutants' office through the back door of the Berghof, or over the terrace." *JRA*

(Left) A wartime summit meeting about the Mediterranean Theater is seen here in the same room, showing, from left to right, Luftwaffe Field Marshal Albert Kesselring, Keitel, Jodl, Hitler, and the Duce in April 1942. The Mediterranean Theater was always Mussolini's primary wartime focus, while the Führer's was always the Eastern Front. Of Hitler's secretaries' office, Junge recalled, "It was a plain, ugly room, only sparsely furnished." *HHA*

(Below) In my opinion, this is the best "Hitler-at-the-map-table" photograph ever taken. From left to right are: Jodl, Halder, the Führer, von Brauchitsch, Keitel, and Schmundt, all hovering over the marble stand in the Grand Salon of FHQ Berghof sometime in 1940–4. Most likely they are planning the secret strike against Stalin's Soviet Union. *HHA*

(Above) A Sherman tank of the American Third Army occupied the Bavarian town of Berchtesgaden below the Berghof on May 4, 1945. Hitler had always said that if the Allies got ashore in France the Third Reich was doomed, and in this he was correct. The tank "was coming from Bischofswiesen to the north," according to Geoff Walden, who visited the sites. *SC*

(Left) Soldiers of the Third U.S. Infantry Division (7th Infantry Regiment) haul down Hitler's swastika banner from the Berghof flagpole before replacing it with the American Stars and Stripes on May 5, 1945. The retreating SS had set the building afire with gasoline the day before. *SC*

(Right) Hitler's daily walk to the Mooslahnerkopf teahouse, 1936. *HHA*

(Below) The Führer (center) listens to Himmler (right) in March 1944 on the Obersalzberg during his daily walk. Generally, the two men discussed SS-related topics during these walks, including the Holocaust, presumably. Behind them at left are SS aide Fritz Darges (left) and SS Gen. Hermann Fegelein. *Walter Frentz*

A good exterior view of the Mooslahnerkopf teahouse (not to be confused with the Kehlsteinhaus). Today, only the steps at left remain. *LC*

(Above) A rare but grainy shot of the teahouse entrance, stone landing, and scenic overlook with birdhouse feeder. *LC*

(Above) The Second Reich Chancellery at Bischofswiesen, Bavaria, not far from the Berghof, in 1937. *LC*

(Left) The reception room in the Second Reich Chancellery. *LC*

(Below) The conference room in the Second RC. *LC*

(Left) The Reich Cabinet Room in the Second RC. The cabinet never convened here, however. *LC*

(Below left) The Führer's office in the Second RC. *LC*

(Bottom) The Second RC also boasted the columns so beloved of all of Hitler's peacetime structures. *LC*

(Above) A good aerial view of the Kehlsteinhaus and its beautiful setting, having escaped the 1951–52 destruction of Nazi buildings. *LC*

(Right) American Army GIs slide open the heavy bronze doors leading into the tunnel that led, in turn, to the elevator shaft up to the Kehlsteinhaus. The tunnel was bored 407 feet into the mountain. *SC*

(Right) GIs at ease in the main hall of the Kehlsteinhaus in May 1945. Note the two chaise lounges brought in from outside. Today, this room is a popular public restaurant open from May through October, run by the Bavarian Alpine Club. *SC*

(Left) In one of only thirteen or fourteen known visits to Kehlsteinhaus—all made during 1939–40—a pensive Führer sits on a chaise lounge on the colonnaded sun terrace on the building's west side. *HHA*

(Below) The Scharitzkehl, or (erronoeusly called) Eva Braun Room, was paneled with rare wood and had two windows that could be lowered to offer a magnificent panoramic view. It was just off the main room. The Gobelin tapestry cost $103,000 in today's dollars. *LC*

(Bottom) The Führer's unused study. *LC*

(Left) The dining room, which could have been used for a military conference but never was. *LC*

As with the Berghof down below, the Kehlsteinhaus offered a marvelous vista from an electronically lowered window, as seen here. *LC*

4 YACHT *AVISO GRILLE*, HOTELS, FÜHRERBAU, AND HRADCANY CASTLE

German Admiralty Yacht *Aviso Grille*

The German admiralty yacht, *Aviso Grille* (translated both as *Cricket* and *Whimsy*), was the Führer's personal, official naval vessel. Its displacement was 2,500 tons, and it had four one-inch guns, two 37mm antiaircraft guns, and four machine guns. It was used for a conference and German fleet review for Hungarian Regent Adm. Miklós Horthy on August 25, 1938.

Wilhelm Keitel recalled in his memoir, *In the Service of the Reich*, about the Czech crisis,

> In August, Halder took the opportunity of a voyage on the Führer's *Grille* on the occasion of a review of the fleet to brief the Führer and myself from a map of his actual operational plan.
>
> The Führer asked numerous questions, but did not express any particular opinion; he asked for a map to be prepared showing all the dispositions and how our forces were to be deployed, and for a brief memorandum on the probable sequence of events. He was particularly interested in those points of the [Czech] enemy's frontier fortifications where it was planned to break through, as he had made a careful study of their value and their weaknesses.
>
> There were a number of differences of opinion on this score, particularly over the use of medium artillery, of which we had only a modest quantity, and over the armored forces and the airborne operations. The briefing conference ended without either a decisive yes or a clear no from him: he wanted to chew it all over again at his leisure.

Added Dr. Dietrich in *Hitler*,

> On board his dispatch boat the *Grille*, from which he witnessed the naval maneuvers near Skaggen, Hitler set sail for Copenhagen and studied the silhouette of the city through his binoculars. . . . He drove frequently to Wilhelmshaven, Hamburg and Kiel to inspect ships and attended launchings. In Hamburg . . . his quarters were always in the Hotel Atlantik on the Alster; he was particularly fond of the tea for which this hotel was famous.

Built at Hamburg's famed Blohm and Voss Shipyards, the *Aviso Grille* was commissioned on May 20, 1935, and used for training duties with destroyers and submarines and as a tender to the Navy's Signal School when not required for the Reich chancellor. With a crew of 248 officers and men, it was 135 meters (147.64 yards) long, had a depth of 4.2 meters (4.59 yards), was powered by a turbine engine, and could attain a speed of 26 knots.

Prior to the war, the official Reich government state yacht was used by Hitler and Raeder for a fleet review in May 1936. In June, it had served as the flagship of Chief Adm. Rolf Carls during North Sea naval maneuvers. The following October, von Blomberg made a trip to the North Cape with a brief stopover at the Norwegian port of Narvik, future scene of the 1940 battle on land and sea. In May 1937, the *Grille* transported von Blomberg again, this time to the coronation of British King George VI in London, and he took an Atlantic cruise the following October. The *Grille* ended 1938 as a target ship for the maneuvers of the torpedo-carrying aircraft of Luftwaffe Squadron 31506. On July 22, 1939, German U-boat fleet commander Adm. Karl Dönitz and his arm's assembled officers aboard the *Grille* were informed by Grand Admiral Dr. Raeder of Hitler's inaccurate prediction that there would be no sea war with the British Royal Navy that year.

It was assigned to the Baltic Station Command at Kiel when the war broke out on September 3, 1939, against the British and French fleets. Then it began operations in laying minefields.

Later, the *Grille* was attached to the Naval Artillery School as a training ship and was to have taken part in Operation Sea Lion to invade the British Isles, but it then spent most of the rest of the war docked in occupied Norwegian waters. Hitler never sailed on it in any known wartime cruise.

The *Grille* was equipped with 78 radio receivers and 103 transmitters, so on its deck at Hamburg newly installed Reich President Dönitz announced Hitler's death to the world on May 1, 1945, a supreme irony. Three days later, it arrived with a German crew in the Scottish Firth of Forth for internment by the enemy and was taken over by the British government.

Oddly, unlike the U.S. Coast Guard cutter *Eagle*—formerly the German naval training ship *Horst Wessel*—the *Grille* was never used in any such capacity, but instead it was broken up in 1951 at Bordentown, New Jersey, after a floating career of but seventeen years. Thus ended the strange saga of Hitler's only known state yacht.

Hotel Excelsior

Both the Führer and his Party rival, Gregor Strasser, stayed here before January 30, 1933, as well as afterward. The Excelsiors were a chain of hotels throughout Germany.

Hotel Elephant, Weimar

In *Hitler's Table Talk, 1941–44*, the Führer recalled,

It was quite an old hotel. . . . I had my usual room, which did have running water, but no bathroom and no lavatory. I had to go down a long corridor and through the last door. . . .When I came out of the smallest room [the toilet] people were giving me ovations, and I had to run the gauntlet back to my own room with my arm raised in salute and a rather embarrassed smile on my face. I had the hotel modernized later.

In *Hitler*, Dr. Dietrich remembered, "Weimar was one of Hitler's regular stopping places. . . . He always stayed in the historic Hotel Elephant, which was later renovated and made into one of the finest hotels in Germany. . . . He regularly attended the performance at the German National Theater, and would afterwards invite the actors and actresses to join him at social gatherings in the lobby of the hotel. Such parties often lasted until dawn.

Hotel Deutscher Hof, Nuremberg

The annual Nazi Party Congresses were held each September at the ancient German city of Nuremberg during the years 1927–38. It was also there that Hitler announced the Nazi Nuremberg Laws against German Jews in 1935. Nuremberg was called the "City of the Party Rallies."

When in Nuremberg, the Führer stayed at the Hotel Deutscher Hof before 1933—when the Grand Hotel across the street refused to admit him—and he thus continued that practice afterward, in Room #s 104 and 105. Dr. Dietrich recalled, "The Deutscher Hof Hotel had a special suite reserved for him. Evenings he liked to sit in its fine, spacious lobby and hobnob with architects and theatrical people."

Just as with the Old Reich Chancellery earlier, the Deutscher Hof soon had its own balcony, upon which Hitler could stand and salute. According to Frederic Spotts in *Hitler and the Power of Aesthetics*, "Balconies became a symbol of Hitler's rule. . . . Never before in history had so many balconies been stood upon so often by a political leader.

Even the existing ornamental balconies of hotels, theaters and opera houses were adapted for his use during his travels around Germany. Looking down upon the crowds, he demonstrated his Führer-ship while inviting popular adulation."

On September 9, 1938, Hitler summoned Generals von Brauchitsch, Halder, and Keitel to the Deutscher Hof during the "First Party Rally of Greater Germany," following his peaceful, diplomatic acquisition of Austria in March 1938. The meeting lasted from midnight to 3:00 AM. Hitler asserted, rightly, that Britain and France would not fight for his next target, the German-populated Sudetenland in Czechoslovakia. He then reviewed Halder's presentation of Case Green—the German Army's code name for the invasion of that country—which Hitler wanted to have completed within one week.

The Führer believed that German howitzers would not be able to smash the sturdy Czech frontier fortifications, and after they had been turned over at the Munich Conference, he was again proved right when a test bombardment of them was conducted. This information was later used to good advantage by the German Army on the parts of the French Maginot Line that were taken by storm.

In 2005 the building still stood, but the balcony had been removed.

The Führerbau at Arcisstrasse #12, Munich

Just north of the Brown House in Munich, the Führerbau (Leader's Building) was built between 1933 and 1937. The Führerbau looks virtually the same today as it did then, except for the missing Nazi eagles and an iron handrail on the front steps has been added for pedestrians. Now a music school, it was constructed to be Hitler's office to accommodate his staff and to hold functions when Hitler was in Munich. Thus, in effect, it succeeded the old Brown House, although both locations were used until 1945.

The Führerbau and an almost identical administrative building, the Verwaltungsbau, on the opposite side of the Briennerstrasse were both designed by Professor Troost, and underground passages connected them. An underground passage also connected the Führerbau to the Brown House. Both the Führerbau and the Verwaltungsbau survived the war virtually undamaged. Today the

Verwaltungsbau houses the Bavarian State Graphics Collection.

The Führerbau faced the Kongisplatz (King's Plaza), which was built by King Ludwig I of Bavaria. According to Brian Deming and Ted Iliff in *Hitler and Munich*, "The granite paving stones that once covered the plaza were ordered by Hitler to serve as a parade site, causing some Munich citizens to dub it the 'Plattensee'—'The Lake of Slabs.'"

Peter Adam, in *Art of the Third Reich*, said that "Hitler was totally involved in the building (of the Führerbau), right to the smallest detail. . . . Almost identical, the two Party buildings consisted of three stories of massive limestone with porticoes, eagles and wreathed swastikas. . . . They also had air-conditioning and huge air raid shelters that linked the two buildings beneath the road." This indicates that as early as 1931, when he planned them, Hitler envisioned the war that he would launch eight years later.

Speer wrote that Hitler insisted that all his building plans be finished by 1950, when he expected that Nazi Germany would have both won World War II and would dominate the globe from the new capital of the Third Reich, Germania, or the former (and current) Berlin.

Hitler and Mussolini met at the Führerbau in September 1937 during the Duce's state visit to Germany. They also met there twice more, the last time being on June 18, 1940, to talk over terms for defeated France. During another visit, they autographed postcards. On one, the Duce wrote, "Men make history," under which Hitler penned, "History makes men."

The Führerbau's main hall was sixty-five feet high and one hundred feet wide, and at each end of the structure were two grand staircases that led to the conference room on the third floor. It had leather-covered walls and a massive marble fireplace, over which was a portrait of Bismarck as well as other paintings and plants.

Dr. Gerdy Troost designed the building's color schemes and wallpaper. The actual room where the Munich Pact was signed is over the south entrance of the Führerbau, facing the Arcisstrasse. Used as a classroom today, it is closed to the public.

The most important wartime meeting at the Führerbau was on May 4, 1943, when the Führer met with Field Marshals von Manstein and Hans-Gunther von Kluge; Col. Gen. Heinz Guderian; and the Luftwaffe's Col. Gen. Hans Jeschonneck. The meeting concerned the postponement of Operation Citadel at Kursk, Russia, until the middle of June, against the advice of all the military men present.

The U.S. Army occupied the Führerbau in 1945.

Hotel Weinzinger, Linz, Austria

According to August Kubizek in *The Young Hitler I Knew*, "On March 12, 1938 . . . on the very spot where his father had once served as a customs official, Hitler crossed the [German-Austrian] frontier. The German Army marched into Austria. . . . Hitler came again to Linz . . . on Apr. 8th—and stayed at the Hotel Weinzinger after a political demonstration at the Kraus locomotive works. . . . The square in front of the hotel was crammed."

It was at the Hotel Weinzinger that Hitler later said he'd decided to annex Austria to Germany outright to form what he called Grossdeutschland, or Greater Germany.

Added Hoffman in *Hitler Was My Friend*, "We went to the Hotel Weinzinger where the officials of the town and the leading Party members were already assembled to welcome us. In a trice, the whole picture altered. 'The private little excursion,' as Hitler called it, was over. The hotel became a headquarters. The telephone rang ceaselessly. . . . Conferences went on until the early hours of the morning. . . . Hitler did not go to bed. . . . Plans were discussed and details arranged for the annexation of Austria and the taking over of the government and the administration. . . . Throughout the night, he kept in constant and close touch with Mussolini," who had sent Italian Army troops to the frontier in 1934 and thus stopped just such an Austrian frolic by the Führer. There was to be no such repeat performance in 1938. Continued Hoffmann, "The floor was covered with all kinds of stuffed wild beasts, and Hitler stumbled two or three times over the head of a Polar bear. . . . Such was the room in which the final negotiations for the incorporation of Austria into the German Reich took place."

Hotel Imperial, Vienna, Austria

Hitler left Vienna in 1913 a penniless, unemployed artist but returned twenty-five years later as the bloodless conqueror of Austria—acclaimed by millions—and established his field FHQ at the Hotel Imperial. There, he accepted the crowd's frenzied adoration from his balcony.

According to Hoffman, "The city's whole two millions seemed jammed on the pavements, and the Hotel Imperial in the Ringstrasse was permanently surrounded by a vast crowd, shouting, 'We want the Führer!' and 'Back to the Homeland!'"

The Hotel Imperial still stands in Vienna and is one of the finest in the city.

Hotel Dreesen, Bad Godesberg, on the Rhine River

At this hotel on the night of June 29–30, 1934, Hitler decided to personally lead the "Blood Purge"—or what later became known as "the national murder weekend"—against his own SA leadership cadre, who were on leave at a Bavarian lakeside villa at Bad Wiessee.

Top SA leaders, it was said, wanted to take over the traditional, professional, Prussian-trained German Army. Hitler, however, knew he would need the Army's support to become the president of Germany after the incumbent, von Hindenburg, died, which occurred on August 2, 1934.

According to Dr. Dietrich in *Hitler*, "At Bad

Godesberg, to which Hitler often proceeded by Rhine steamer from Mainz or Coblenz on fine summer days, the Hotel Dreesen was his regular headquarters. Rudolf Hess . . . had recommended this hotel to him, and in the early years of his struggle for power, he had often stopped there. Later, he kept to his habit. His rooms looked out over the Rhine, and at coffee time he often drove out to the Petersberg."

The second Hitler-Chamberlain summit conference over the Südetenland crisis took place at the Hotel Dreesen on September 22, 1938. Noted John Toland in *Adolf Hitler*, "Hitler greatly admired the view from the restaurant—he often came up at coffee time. . . . From his balcony [at the Hotel Peterburg at Königswinter am Rhein] Chamberlain could look across the river at the Dreesen." The talks stalemated as Hitler demanded immediate German occupation of the Südetenland, and Chamberlain went home. War looked imminent until the Munich Pact provided a brief reprieve.

Hradcany Castle, Prague, Czechoslovakia

After the fall of Czechoslovakia, Hitler spent the night of March 15–16, 1939, in the famed Hradcany Castle in Prague, in Nazi-occupied Bohemia and Moravia. As SS chauffeur Col. Erich Kempka wrote in his postwar memoir, *I Burned Hitler*, "The next day [March 16], Hitler was introduced to some generals and government officials. We were not well protected, and when I think back, it would have been easy for the Czechs to take us prisoner."

(Below left) A good stern view of Hitler's yacht *Aviso Grille* (often abbreviated to *Grille*). HHA *(Below right)* A good side view of the *Grille*. HHA *(Bottom)* On August 25, 1938, at the German naval station at Kiel, the Führer and his guests aboard the *Grille* review the U-boat fleet. From left to right are: Hitler, Hungarian Regent Adm. Miklós Horthy, German Army Commander in Chief Colonel General von Brauchitsch, Admiral Raeder, and Colonel General Keitel. *Walter Frentz*

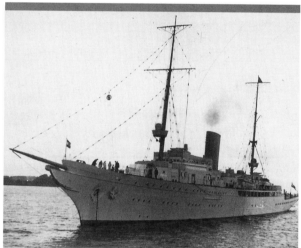

(Left) In this previously unpublished photo, Hitler gives an informal Nazi salute next to chauffeur SS man Julius Schreck in 1935, as their Mercedes-Benz open touring car pulls up in front of one of several Hotel Excelsiors across Nazi Germany. Hitler stayed in several such hotels during both his drive for national office before 1933 and his consolidation of it afterward. His Party rival, Gregor Strasser, also stayed at an Excelsior. Note the name over the doorway. *HHA*

(Above) Hitler and Hess review passing SS troops in front of the Haus Elephant (Hotel) at Weimar, 1936. Note the elephant above the hotel's marquee. *HHA*

The Führer (center, at the open window of the Deutscher Hof) is serenaded by an Army band at the end of the September 1934 Nuremberg Nazi Party Congress. This room was "on the first floor (second floor to Americans)." *HHA*

(Above) A closer view of the same window, with Hitler's name lit up in lightbulbs (also seen in the previous photo). *HHA*

(Left) Just as the Old RC had, the Deutscher Hof soon had its own special Führer balcony. An open french door is behind the saluting Hitler. The Führerstandarte is on the hotel's façade at upper right, over the doorway. *HHA*

(Below) Another angle of the same scene, showing Hitler's view of the street below. *HHA*

(Right) An August 2005 view of the Deutscher Hof next to the opera (left). At the time this was taken, the hotel was closed for renovations. Note, too, that the Führer's former balcony has vanished. *J. Cowdery*

(Above) In this previously unpublished photo, a massive German bronze eagle with a Nazi swastika in its talons is hauled into place and affixed to the Führerbau, overlooking the left balcony. *HHA*

(Right) A good view of the left of the two balconies on the front of the Führerbau, with one Nazi eagle facing inward and right and its mate on the other balcony facing inward and left, thus toward each other. *HHA*

(Left) A good, wide-angle view of the entire Führerbau (Hitler's office building), showing two of its four balconies. *HHA*

(Above) One of the two beautiful marble grand staircases as it looks now. *Steven Lehrer*

(Above) Mussolini (left) and Hitler in the Führerbau during Mussolini's state visit to Germany in September 1937. *HHA*

(Right) In this previously unpublished photograph, one of the grand staircases is seen in use on June 18, 1940; from left to right on the ground level are: Count Ciano, von Ribbentrop, and an SS aide. In the next group up are, left to right, the Italian ambassador to Germany, Dino Alfieri and the German ambassador to Italy, Georg von Mackensen. *JRA*

(Above) A previously unpublished view of Nazi aides carrying maps and documents in one of the Führerbau's marbled halls on June 18, 1940, for the Nazi-Fascist discussions on armistice conditions for defeated France. *JRA*

(Right) A good view of one of the Führerbau's hallways. *HHA*

(Above) With Dr. Göbbels (left) and Nazi publisher Maz Armann (to the left of Göbbels) at his side, Chancellor Hitler delivers an impassioned speech to Nazi editors on the day after Kristallnacht—November 11, 1938—in the Führerbau's main reception room on the first floor. The Führer also used this room for formal press conferences. It was richly paneled with rare wood and nine massive tapestries celebrating the deeds of Hercules. Hitler's own office walls were covered with red leather. Today, it is the school's concert hall. *HHA*

(Above) The Führerbau's living room, designed by Dr. Gerdy Troost and architect Leonard Gall, featuring *The Four Elements* (seen here) by artist Adolf Ziegler. According to Spotts in *Hitler and the Power of Aesthetics,* "The French Ambassador [André François-Poncet] said it should've been called *The Four Senses*—since taste was lacking. . . .' Adolf Ziegler disgraced himself in 1943 by recommending peace negotiations; the painting was removed." *Signal Magazine*

(Above) The actual room, Hitler's personal Führerbau office, where the Munich Pact talks of September 29–30, 1938, with Germany, Italy, France, and Great Britain were conducted. A portrait of Bismarck hangs above the mantelpiece. The fate of dismembered Czechoslovakia was decided here in a few short hours; today the room is a classroom. Later, waving the piece of paper that Hitler had signed in his apartment afterward, Chamberlain boasted that he'd come to England bringing "peace in our time." Hitler told von Ribbentrop instead, "But don't take it so seriously. That piece of paper is of no significance whatever." *LC*

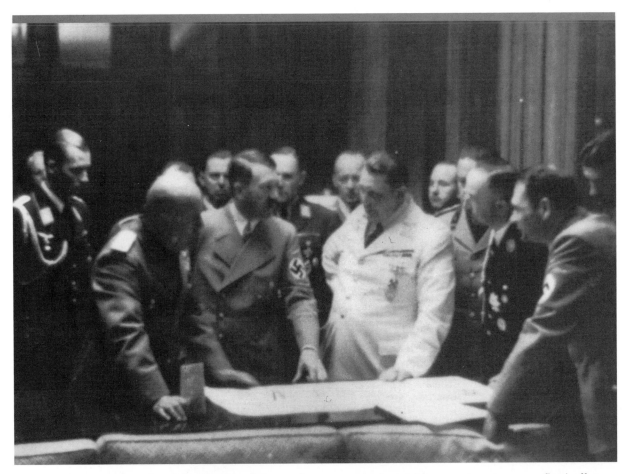

(Above) The second and middle session of the conference started at 4:30 PM and was a more fluid affair, with people breaking up into informal groups, as in this previously unpublished photograph, around a map of the disputed area. From left to right are: Ernst von Weizacker of the German Foreign Office, von Below, Mussolini, unknown official, Schaub, Hitler, Bodenschatz, unknown official, Göring, Dr. Otto Dietrich, Ciano, Himmler, Hess, and Hitler's Motor Corp (NSKK) adjutant Capt. Fritz Wiedemann. Alto-

gether, the Munich Conference lasted thirteen hours. *HHA*

(Right) A weary Count Ciano and French Premier Edouard Daladier lounge on the couch in front of the fireplace during the third and final session of the Munich Conference. The signing of the pact was over by 2:30 AM, and the Czechs were informed that their fate had been settled without them. *HHA*

(Above left) Hitler's cross-country Mercedes-Benz G-4 open touring car pulls up at the Hotel Weinzinger in Linz, Austria, on April 8, 1938, as seen in this previously unpublished photograph. SS Colonel Kempka is driving. *HHA*

(Above right) Hitler (right) on the balcony of FHQ Hotel Imperial on Vienna's Ringstrasse near the Opera on March 14, 1938. The building still stands. *Walter Frentz*

(Left) A recent photograph of the Hotel Imperial in Vienna. In the previous photograph, the Führer stood on the balcony on top of the second floor at the center of the building. It was here that he proclaimed the creation of the Greater German Reich with the inclusion of Austria and that the nation's Cardinal, Theodor Innitzer, who expressed his support, also visited him. *Steven Lehrer*

(Right) Hitler (right) approaches the Hotel Dreesen on the Rhine River by steamer in 1933. During the years 1925–33, hotel owner Fritz Dreesen allowed Hitler to stay there for free. In honor of the Führer's Bad Godesberg talks with Chamberlain, he refurnished and recarpeted the hotel completely to further please Hitler, who made it his headquarters for the meeting. The British prime minister stayed across the river at the Hotel Petersburg. *HHA*

(Above) Hitler sees his guest to the main entrance of the Hotel Dreesen. From left to right are: Chamberlain, Dr. Schmidt, Hitler, and aide Albert Bormann. Just prior to this picture being taken, Hoffmann had taken another of the two leaders near a palm tree in the lobby, calling it "The Palm of Peace." *HHA*

(Right) On March 16, 1939, Hitler made a symbolic appearance from a window of the Hradcany Castle to show that he was now the ruler of a pair of former dynastic imperiums, those of the Hohenzollerns and the Habsburgs. He had arrived by car at midnight on the fifteenth, according to SS valet Heinz Linge in *Until the Fall*. *HHA*

(Left) The Führer stayed but a single night in Prague, March 15–16, 1939, and never returned. Here (center) he confers with his SS minions, Reinhard Heydrich (left) and Himmler (second from left), who set up typical Nazi police state rule in the city and the country forthwith. *HHA*

(Left) Inside Hradcany Castle, discussing the technical problems of the occupation of Bohemia and Moravia are, from left to right, unknown officer; Gens. Wilhelm Keitel (hand to mouth), Heinrich von Stulpnagel, and Johannes Blaskowitz; Hitler; and another unidentified officer inside, possibly Engel. *HHA*

(Left) The new ruler of Bohemia and Moravia, Hitler (right), meets at the Hradcany Castle with the former head of the Czech state, President Dr. Emil Hácha, whom the Germans maintained in office right up until 1945. *HHA*

5 THE NEW REICH CHANCELLERY

At the end of January 1938, Hitler ordered Albert Speer to start construction of the New German Reich Chancellery in Berlin. This new, grand chancellery would supersede the creaky Old Reich Chancellery. Hitler wanted it finished in time for the annual New Year's Diplomatic Reception to be held on January 9, 1939, the year that the Führer expected to launch his first war in Europe. Speer presented the finished building to a grateful Hitler two days ahead of the announced schedule. In the coming weeks, Hitler invited all the foreign diplomats, his generals and admirals, and all Nazi Party gauleiters (regional leaders) and Reichsleiters (national leaders) to see and tour his new pride and joy, and come they did.

The entire building faced the Voss Strasse. It was 442 meters (483.83 yards) in length and shaped like a giant horseshoe with a pair of wings and its main section at the back. This New Reich Chancellery had three floors and was built in identical neo-classical styling to that of the Munich Party buildings. Its main entrance fronted the Wilhelmsplatz as before, and classical pillars encompassed a courtyard 26 meters wide and 48 meters (52.5 yards) deep. Inside, there were many halls and ballrooms, principally the 46-meter-long Mosaikshalle (Mosaic Hall), so called because of its many wall mosaics. There was also a 16-meter-high Runder Saal (Round Hall), plus the 146-meter Long Hall that was 12 meters wide. The Führer's personal office measured 27 by 14.5 meters and was 10 meters high (29.53 by 15.86 yards and 10.94 yards high). Hitler's initials were mounted atop the main entrance doorway, which was guarded by a pair of black-clad SS sentries armed with rifles with fixed bayonets.

A giant reception hall measured 24.5 meters (26.79 yards) long and 16.5 wide (18.04 yards), and there was another where the Reich Cabinet was supposed to meet but never actually did. Many other meetings were held there, however. A small army of 4,500 men and women had worked day and night to raise the building, and the interior marble came from areas all across the Third Reich.

Cost was no object to Hitler and Speer in the building's construction, and it was indeed the most expensive and luxurious of all such structures in Nazi Germany. The building was designed partly to impress the population with the might and majesty of Hitler's regime as well as the idea that it would last forever, or at least a thousand years. In the end, it endured but sixteen.

The war that Hitler began on September 1, 1939, doomed not only him and his regime in general, but it also reduced the New Reich Chancellery to rubble and ashes by the end of the global conflict.

The Führerbunker underneath was Hitler's last refuge, the location of his suicide, and enemy soldiers from both fronts had their pictures snapped by the overturned marble map table in his private study. Red Army architects recycled the expensive building materials to build their own war memorial in Berlin-Treptow, and the precious rouge marble clad the inside of a Berlin subway section as well, where it can still be seen today.

No Dissent by Hitler's Marshals and Generals on the Launching of the Russian Campaign, March 30, 1941, at the New Reich Chancellery

No major campaign in military history was ever started with such a poor assessment of the potential enemy forces. The initial estimate in the summer of 1940 of 155 Red Army divisions was upped to 247 by April 1941, but by August—with the assault already fully advanced—the true figure was finally known: fully 366 enemy divisions!

The Führer had foolishly bitten off more than he could chew, much less digest. Stalin panicked at first, but in the end, he pulled himself together sufficiently to wage the most ruthless land war in history to date.

Despite what they said, testified, and wrote after the lost war against the USSR, the Führer's field marshals and generals failed to protest the coming war and its barbarities against Communist Russian commissars (shot on sight), Jews, Gypsies, and others (killed in cold blood as "partisans" behind the lines). According to one of their own, Walter Warlimont, writing in 1964 in *Inside Hitler's Headquarters*:

The first occasion on which Hitler openly demanded unlawful action from the Wehrmacht was on March 30, 1941. On that date he made

73

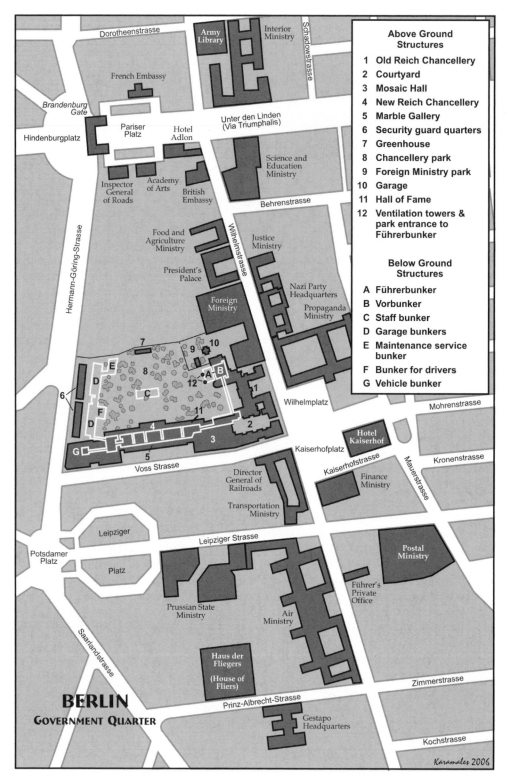

Berlin Government Quarter. *Map by Jay Karamales. © Potomac Books, Inc.*

a speech lasting almost 2 ½ hours to some 200–250 senior officers, consisting of the Commanders-in-Chief of the three Services and the senior Army, Navy and Air Force commanders selected for the Eastern campaign together with their senior staff officers.

The meeting took place in a large conference room at the Ebertsrasse [sic] end of the Great Hall of the Reich Chancellery; the hall was entirely full and those present were seated in long rows of chairs according to rank and seniority.... They sat there before him in stubborn silence, a silence broken only twice—when the assembly rose first as he entered through a door in the rear and went up to the rostrum, and later when he departed the same way. Otherwise, not a hand moved and not a word was spoken other than by him.

No objections were made, no questions were asked, and—as Warlimont concluded—"Hitler's intentions were forgotten in a conspiracy of silence." But they were recalled by the victorious Allies during the war crimes trials of 1945–49 and thereafter.

Defeated by the Allies Instead, 1941–45

The Red Army defeated the German Army across the board in every way possible: leadership, numbers, strategy, tactics, weaponry, deployment, and endurance. In the end, Hitler tried to rally the German people around his capital in 1945—as Stalin had done with the Soviets at Moscow four years earlier—and failed yet again. With that loss came the end of the war and his own demise.

When he returned to the New RC in January 1945, Hitler ran the hopeless war from his formerly grand office, as described by Capt. Gerhard Boldt in *Hitler: The Last Ten Days*: "An elaborate marble map table stood halfway along the wall, its black, upholstered chair placed so that Hitler could look out on to the park. On the map table there was only a telephone, an electric bell, two unusually heavy paperweights, a desk set and a few colored pencils. The only other objects in the room were a heavy, round table, massive leather armchairs and a couch, arranged along the left and right walls."

Hitler lost the war, and in the process he destroyed the German Armed Forces and their former guiding light, the General Staff, which ceased to exist in 1945. He fired its chief, Colonel General Guderian, on March 28, 1945, following a heated argument, and on April 1 its last chief, Gen. Hans Krebs, was appointed in his stead. By then, the daily military situation conferences had moved from the New RC Führer's Office into the confines of the Führerbunker, the thirteenth and final FHQ.

The Old RC–New RC complex had been bombed by the Allies in January and again in early February 1945.

Time-Life Books called this model "A Workplace Fit for a Führer," and it is easy to see why. The model shows the huge New RC (left) combined with the Old RC (right). The Voss Strasse bordered the left side, while the Wilhelmstrasse intersected it at lower right. The wide open area at the left rear was the park for the entire complex, often referred to as the Reich Chancellery garden. Hitler and other top Nazis liked to take walks in the spacious park area. Note also the Honor Courtyard, which is visible in the lower center portion of the photo. *HHA*

In *Hitler and the Power of Aesthetics*, Frederic Spotts stated, "The [New RC] building was largely intact, but a burned out hulk," after fifty-eight heavy bombs detonated in the area of the Chancellery alone. The diplomats and generals of old had been replaced in 1945, and Kempka asserted in *I Burned Hitler*: "Rooms in the Chancellery were used as hospitals, due to the constant arrival of the wounded."

The Red Army's 284th and 301st Rifle Divisions led the final assault on the Reich Chancellery complex, which they took after fierce, close-in combat both outside and within the buildings. Red Army political commissar Maj. Anna Nikulina of the Ninth Rifle Corps was singled out by Marshal Georgi Zhukov—conqueror of Nazi Berlin—for special commendation, after she climbed to the roof with a Red flag beneath her jacket and tied it to the very flagpole of Hitler's former Führerstandarte with a piece of telephone wire.

And what of Hitler's ornate, grandiose New German Reich Chancellery in Berlin? Today, it has completely vanished, replaced with hundreds of units of cheaply built apartments.

(Left) A pair of white-belted LSSAH guards stand at show arms out the New RC. *Signal Magazine*

(Above left) A front, aerial view of the demolished New Reich Chancellery in the rubble of 1945 Berlin, as seen from the Wilhelmstrasse at the Honor Courtyard entrance. The door to the main building is visible at the rear at the far end of the Honor Courtyard. The Speer balcony can be seen to the right of the Honor Courtyard doorway, on the second level just above the street rubble. *SC*

(Above right) Looking at the same building from the air and from the opposite end (right). In the foreground is the ornamental pool outside Hitler's office. One has to look closely to find it, but the Führerbunker's emergency exit is to the left and directly upward: the small, square building with the black door in the center, just before the next open space and the two-story building behind that. The Hitlers were burned and buried to the front and right of the exit as the photo is viewed. *SC*

(Bottom) The small, garage-like, square building at center left—to the left of the larger building with the gaping hole in its roof—was the emergency exit from the two bunkers beneath. *SC*

(Left) This is a corner of the Propaganda Ministry on March 14, 1945. *HHA*

(Below) "Crowned with the emblem of the Great German Empire (Reich): the west portal of the New RC in the Voss Strasse," #6 entrance, as noted in the official guidebook. The building was dedicated January 10, 1939, when the Führer officially took up residence therein. The following May 23, Hitler told the general staff at the New RC that he would take not only Danzig but Poland as well if it was necessary to get what he wanted. Here, two white-belted, black-clad members of the Lifeguard SS Adolf Hitler Regiment stand guard on the steps. *Signal Magazine.*

(Right) The Honor Courtyard entrance (left) through the Old Reich Chancellery annex with the Speer balcony at right on the second floor. Wrote Richard Raiber in *After the Battle* in 1977, "Speer retained the old (1929–30) extension [seen here], but cut a large double doorway—wide enough for vehicles— as the entrance to the Ehrenhof (Honor Courtyard)." The huge bronze doors measured eleven-and-a-half by twenty-three feet. *HHA*

(Below) The same side of the building, seen in 1945. *SC*

(Above) The same scene on April 19, 1939, during a parade the night before Hitler's fiftieth birthday. The Speer balcony is at right and the double-door entrance at left. *HHA*

(RIght) A wartime scene on the balcony of the Reich Chancellery annex. In this previously unpublished photo are, from left to right: Keitel, Labor Corps Leader Konstantin Hierl, Dr. Göbbels, Martin Bormann, Göring, Hitler, Hess, von Ribbentrop, Frick, unknown man, Raeder, Dr. Ley, and von Brauchitsch. *JRA*

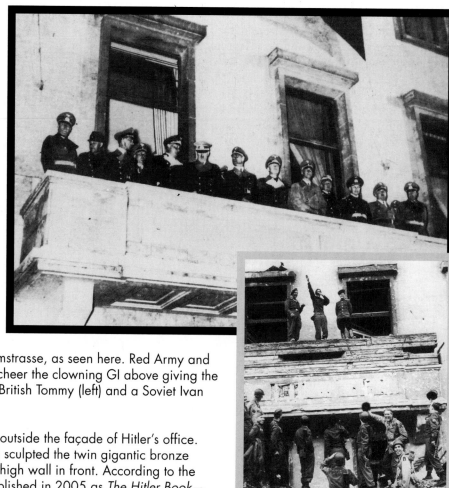

(Far right) During the Battle of Berlin in 1945, the famous balcony was fortified as a firing post to cover the Wilhelmsplatz and Wilhelmstrasse, as seen here. Red Army and U.S. Army soldiers below cheer the clowning GI above giving the Hitler salute, flanked by a British Tommy (left) and a Soviet Ivan (right). *SC*

(Below) The New RC park outside the façade of Hitler's office. Josef Thorak (1889–1952) sculpted the twin gigantic bronze horses at either end of the high wall in front. According to the Soviet report to Stalin—published in 2005 as *The Hitler Book*—the New RC cost 88.9 million marks to build. For one, "because of the swampy subsoil, the Chancellery was built on a concrete raft." *HHA*

(Left) British Prime Minister Winston Churchill walking in the ruins on the park side, atop the wall of the plaza, outside the Führer's office (at left) on July 16, 1945. *USNA*

(Below) An architectural model of the Honor Courtyard that shows the opposite end from the photograph below, the one toward which all visitors headed. The two statues were sculpted by Arno Breke; the one at the left was called *The Party*, with a torch in hand, and the one at right, *The Armed Forces*, with a sword. From the front door at the Honor Courtyard (which led to the entrance hall, where liveried servants in powdered wigs and blue satin jackets awaited) to Hitler's office door was a walk of nearly 250 yards, more than two full-size American football fields. *HHA*

(Above) The Führer (left, center) reviews men of the Nazi Labor Service (right) in the marble Honor Courtyard of the New RC in the spring of 1939 with, from left to right, Dr. Ley, Bruckner, Sepp Dietrich, and Heydrich. The man at Hitler's left is the commander of the unit being reviewed. The doors at the rear are those facing the Wilhelmstrasse that allowed motorcades bearing foreign diplomats and Army generals into the Chancellery. The giant doors at the rear are closed. *Walter Frentz*

(Right) A good close-up of the statue *The Party* outside the main doorway of the New RC, and inside the Honor Courtyard in 1939. *HHA*

(Below) Inside the Honor Courtyard in May 1945, as Red Army soldiers tour the debris-littered ruins. *LC*

(Above) Red Army Marshal Georgi Zhukov (front, third from left) and his staff stroll across the captured Honor Courtyard toward the double doors on May 5, 1945, the day his troops stormed the building and took it from the Lifeguard SS Adolf Hitler Division, among other defending forces. *LC*

(Above) An Allied view of the same spot in 1945, with only the outline of the missing eagle visible over the doorway. What happened to it? *SC*

(Above left) On January 10, 1939—following the annual New Year's Diplomatic Reception—Hitler (center) takes his leave of the New RC, followed by, from left to right: von Ribbentrop, Brückner, and Keitel. This is the main entrance to the New RC off of the Honor Courtyard, completed by Speer just two days before. Note the faces of the white-belted Lifeguard SS Adolf Hitler Regiment sentries, as they nervously eye the Führer's departure. The bronze Nazi eagle above the doorway was sculpted by Kurt Schmid-Ehmen. *JRA*

(Left) Here is what happened to the eagle: Red Army soldiers load the dethroned Nazi eagle from the doorway onto a waiting truck for shipment to Moscow. The same eagle has been on display ever since in the Central Museum of the Soviet Armed Forces, along with captured battle flags (left) of the vanquished German Army. *LC*

(Right) The Führer's ornate Cabinet Room in the New RC, with furnishings designed by Dr. Gerdy Troost and Prof. Gall and their United Munich Workshops, which also furnished Hitler's residences. Hitler avoided using his cabinet by issuing orders directly to the ministries. No cabinet meetings were ever held again after 1937. While Hitler never used this room for cabinet meetings, he did use it for other purposes. Von Below recalled in *At Hitler's Side*, "On March 30, 1941,

Hitler summoned the Wehrmacht [Armed Forces] leaders to his Cabinet office, where he delivered a 2 ½-hour speech in which he declared, 'What has to be achieved in Russia is the destruction of the Red Army and Soviet state. . . . It is a war of extermination!'" *Signal Magazine*

(Below right) Another view of the Cabinet Room, but this time from behind Hitler's own chair at the head of the conference table, in July 1939. The following November 5—in a stormy session at the New RC—von Brauchitsch tried to resign his command of the Army

over the Führer's insistence that the attack in the west be launched that month instead of waiting until the winter or spring of 1940. Hitler refused to accept the resignation for political reasons, but from then on von Brauchitsch was a marked man, or in Hitler's eyes, a defeatist. Hitler fired him on December 19, 1941, partially as a result of the so-called Spirit of Zossen. *HHA*

(Above left) Breker's sculpture, *The Genius*, was atop this seventeen-foot-high doorway to the Runder Saal (Round Hall) of the New RC, which boasted walls of priceless red marble, as seen here. *Signal Magazine*

(Above right) On November 12, 1940, in this previously unpublished photo, a Soviet delegation led by People's Foreign Commissar Vyacheslav M. Molotov (center)—flanked by the Soviet ambassador to Berlin, Vladimir Dekanozov (left), and Meissner (right), and followed by Schaub (left), von Puttkamer, and German Protocol Chief Baron Alexander von Dornberg (right)—enters the Round Hall from the opposite end. Note Breker's sculpture, *The Warrior*, above the doorway. Five years later, Molotov, Soviet NKVD (security) Chief Lavrenti P. Beria, and possibly Stalin himself revisited the same site, then in ruins. *JRA*

(Bottom left) The same room in July 1945, destroyed, and being toured by a British Tommy and a GI after the war. *The Genius* is still visible atop one of the two doorways. *SC*

(Right) The Soviet delegation and its hosts enter the Mosaic Hall from the Round Hall in this previously unpublished photograph. *JRA*

(Below) Another view of the Mosaic Hall. The eagle had been the national symbol of Germany since Charlemagne in 800 AD, and Hitler merely added his Party's symbol, the swastika, in 1933. Today it is the Imperial War Museum in London. *Signal Magazine*

(Right) The Mosaic Hall as it looked to Hitler upon unveiling on January 7, 1939. After the war, the Red Army Memorial at Berlin-Treptow received much of the precious marble, as did the new Berlin subway's interior walls. Note the glass skylight above that provided light in the otherwise windowless room. *LC*

(Left) The state funerals of both Fritz Todt and Heydrich were held in the Mosaic Hall. Here, on April 19, 1939, the Führer (left) received more than 1,600 top Nazi officials who wished him a happy fiftieth birthday for the morrow. Facing him in the front rank, from left to right, are: three unknown men after the flag bearers at far left, Dr. Philip Bouhler, Alfred Rosenberg, Max Amann, Walter Buch, Schwarz, Frank, Frick, Martin Bormann, Dr. Ley, Dr. Göbbels, and Hitler Youth Leader Baldur von Schirach. Following the state funeral of SA Staff Chief Viktor Lutze in the Mosaic Hall on May 7, 1943, Hitler took the opportunity to address the assembled Party gauleiters concerning the losses at Stalingrad and other matters. *HHA*

(Above) Göring (left, holding his Luftwaffe field marshal's baton) wishes the Führer (right) a happy fiftieth birthday on April 20, 1939, in the New RC's Great Reception Hall. Here Hitler also addressed his assembled field marshals and generals on other occasions. *HGA*

(Left) Recalled Speer in *Inside the Third Reich*, "On my flight to see Hitler for the last time on Apr, [*sic*] 23, 1945, I wanted once more to walk through the Chancellery I had built. . . ." This is what was left of the wrecked hulk of the formerly magnificent Mosaic Hall after the war—"the skylight shattered, the walls stripped bare and the floor covered with rubble." *SC*

(Right) The very same room—in a previously unpublished shot—under Russian occupation in 1945. *HST*

(Below) A good, wide-angle view of the Marble Gallery (also referred to as the "Long Hall" because of its length of more than five hundred feet) leading to Hitler's own office, the tall doorway on the right. The Wall of Windows at left looked out onto the Voss Strasse. *Signal Magazine*—the official publication of the wartime German Armed Forces—stated, "The 'Long Hall' in the New RC. . . . The bright walls are made of marble stucco. Between the doors which lead to the Führer's Study [right] and the room of the aide-de-camp [farther down on the same side], the walls are hung with Gobelins [tapestries]. Beautifully shaped tables and chairs together with gilded wall sconces of bronze give the gallery, in spite of its size, a harmonious character." The surface of the floor was very slippery, and Hitler was delighted that foreign statesmen would have difficulty keeping their footing when they came to see him. *Signal Magazine*

(Above) On May 22, 1939, the Pact of Steel—a formal military alliance—was signed by representatives of Nazi Germany and Fascist Italy in the New RC. It helped bring on World War II less than one hundred days later. Seen here, walking down the Marble Gallery and returning from the signing ceremony are, from left to right: von Ribbentrop (obscured), Prof. Hoffmann, unknown official, Schaub, Count Ciano, two unidentified aides, the Führer, German Ambassador to Rome von Mackensen, two Italian officers, von Dornberg, Göring, two unknown men, Keitel, Brückner, SS interpreter Eugen Dollmann, Dr. Meissner, and Sepp Dietrich. Note the special gold-braided belt that Hitler wore for the occasion. *JRA*

(Left) The very same hallway in 1945—looking in the opposite direction—but a shadow of its former self. *LC*

The view from behind Hitler's desk, looking toward the other end of the vast room, with the twin entry doors from the Marble Gallery at the right. Over the fireplace at center is the famed full-length portrait of Bismarck by Franz von Lenbach, and at far left is the marble map table with ornate lamps and a small, white marble equestrian statue of Hitler's hero, King Frederick II (the Great) of Prussia. To the left of the map table were the five tall french doors that led out to the broad plaza and wall overlooking the park. Here is how *Signal Magazine* described this mammoth office: "The heart of the New Chancellery is a room 90 feet long, nearly 50 feet wide and nearly 33 feet high. The walls are composed of dark red marble from the Eastern Marches and the wainscoting is of dark brown ebony. The floor is made of marble." Just prior to leaving the New RC to review his four-hour, fiftieth-birthday parade on April 20, 1939, Hitler told his assembled service commanders from behind this desk that there would most likely be war with the Western powers within the next few years, a sobering thought for all of them. Over the doors leading into this colossal room, Speer had optimistically situated Plato's four virtues: Wisdom, Fortitude, Temperance, and Justice. As recently as 1994, the desk itself was still intact in Munich. *Signal Magazine*

(Below) A 1939 edition of *Signal Magazine* stated, "The door to the Führer's Study. It is 20 feet high, made of mahogany and German [red] marble, and decorated with the initials AH [with oak leaves, overtop, in a cartouche by Hans Vogel]. The huge door connects the Führer's Study with the 'Long Hall,' guarded by a pair of white-strappinged, black-uniformed members of his elite Lifeguard SS Adolf Hitler Bodyguard Regiment." *Signal Magazine*

(Top and Above) A comparative view of the same scene in 1945—original room at top and the destroyed room above—with the overturned map table at left and the globe's support piece at the far right doorway at the end of the office. In *Inside the Third Reich*, Speer recalled the dedication on January 10, 1939: "His study met with his undivided approval. He was particularly pleased by the inlay on his desk representing a sword half drawn from its sheath, 'Good, good! When the diplomats sitting in front of me see that, they'll learn to shiver and shake!'" *SC*

(Left) A view of how a visitor saw the Führer's desk. He would enter his office by the rear door, seen here, while visitors came in through the main double doors to his right. In the right corner is the previously never-noted bust of von Hindenburg, whom Hitler admired to his dying day as "Der Alte Herr" (the old gentleman). At left is a seventeenth-century tapestry. The desk had a trio of panels emblazoned on its front (from left to right): "Gorgon, whose glance turns the beholder to stone; Mars, god of war, with his sword; and Minerva, goddess of war. The cartouche over the door—portraying a knight with Hitler's face being pursued by Death and the Devil, symbolizes fearlessness," according to *Signal Magazine. HHA*

(Below) Almost the exact angle from which a visitor would have approached the Führer's desk from the main entrance, after having crossed the broad expanse of carpet to reach it. *Signal Magazine*

(Right) In its first publication this photograph is of a historic event that took place in the Führer's ornate office in the New RC in the early hours of March 15, 1939, as the remainder of the former Czechoslovak states of Bohemia and Moravia was surrendered to the Third Reich by its president, Dr. Emil Hácha. Seen here from left to right are: Dr. Hácha's aide, Dr. Hácha in animated conversation with the Reich chancellor, Göring, von Ribbentrop, Keitel, and von Weizacker. Dr. Hácha suffered a mild heart attack after Göring threatened to flatten Prague with his Luftwaffe bombers. Once he revived, the president signed away his country's independence. At far left is the map table with the equestrian statue of Frederick the Great, and at right are the closed drapes of the study's french doors. *HGA*

(Far right) A conference in Hitler's New RC office on March 23, 1939, after the Germans occupied Prague and the rest of Bohemia and Moravia the week before. From left to right, around the table: Meissner (back to camera), obscured man, Slovakian President Father Josef Tiso (third from left), Hitler (right), and Keitel (far right), who also has his back to the lens. *HHA*

(Right) Another view from behind Hitler's desk, looking toward the other end of the room. Here, on April 20, 1939, the Führer (left) received fiftieth-birthday greetings from his High Command, from left center to right in this previously unpublished photograph: Göring (Air Force), Raeder (Navy), von Brauchitsch (Army), and Keitel (OKW). *HGA*

(Above) On August 13 or 14, 1940 (accounts differ), the Führer is seen here in his office with his assembled Army field marshals. The latter had just been presented with their batons of office, which were granted to them in Hitler's Reichstag speech of July 19. From left to right are: Keitel, von Rundstedt, Fedor von Bock, Reich Marshal Göring, Hitler, von Brauchitsch, Wilhelm Leeb, Wilhelm List, Hans-Gunther von Kluge, Erwin von Witzleben, and von Reichenau. *HGA*

(Left) On June 9, 1942, the Führer (far right) again received Dr. Emil Hácha, president of German-occupied Czechoslovakia (Bohemia and Moravia only). From left to right are: two members of Hácha's government, SS Gen. Kurt Daluege, a trio of other Czech officials, Dr. Meissner, Hácha, Dr. Lammers, and Hitler. The occasion was the state funeral of Heydrich in the Mosaic Hall, following his assassination in Prague. *HHA*

(Left) Taken in July 1939, an excellent close-up of the pristine marble map table and statue of King Frederick the Great in Hitler's New RC office. Through the french doors is the Orangerie (Winter Garden) across the RC park. *HHA*

(Right) Another 1945 view—and one unpublished before now—of the Führer's former ornate office, looking left toward the overturned marble map table and shattered french door. *HST*

(Below) A good close-up view of the formerly grand, but now overturned, marble map table, complete with a trio of females from the American Women's Army Corps (WACs) and a cigarette-smoking Red Army Ivan. *HST*

(Right) In a scene just outside the french doors of his office, Hitler is seen feeding a squirrel in the park of the Old RC–New RC complex in the spring of 1939. In the background are the doors of the Orangerie. Dr. Dietrich recalled in *Hitler*, "In the Chancellery park, Hitler ruthlessly ordered the cutting down of the venerable oaks and beaches [*sic*] which Bismarck had loved. The trees had grown infirm, but a great many people were sorry to see them go. In their place, Hitler had a fountain and pool constructed in the middle of the lawn. On the other hand, he fed the squirrels which made their way over from the nearby Tiergarten and trustfully came almost to the door of the apartment. No Providence and no sixth sense warned him in these promising years of peace that only a few years later he himself would find his grave among the roots of those historic trees, roots churned up by bombs and shells." *HHA*

(Above) The dining room of the New RC in July 1939. The windows looked out on the park, and in 1945, machine guns bristled from them. *HHA*

(Left) The Führer (center) with architect Prof. Hermann Giesler (left) and Dr. Ley (right) on February 9, 1945, viewing a model of Linz, Austria, in the entrance area of the Führerbunker at the New RC. According to Spotts in *Hitler and the Power of Aesthetics*, Hitler told fellow Austrian and SS Gen. Ernst Kaltenbrunner, "If I were not convinced that you and I will rebuild the city of Linz according to these plans, I would put a bullet through my head this very day!" *HHA*

(Right) A final look at the Linz architectural model on February 9, 1945. *Walter Frentz*

(Below) One of the last two known pictures of Hitler alive, both taken with Schaub (left) on April 21, 1945, the day after his fifty-sixth and final birthday. He was inspecting the ruins of the Chancellery complex, just nine days before his suicide. This picture is famous, but I have been unable to pinpoint the exact locations of either this picture or the next within the RC complex. In the summer of 1950, the final remains of the building above ground were blown up and covered with dirt in what was then Communist East Berlin. Debris was still being trucked away in 1956, eleven years after the end of the war. *HHA*

(Above) The very last known photo of Hitler alive, with Schaub. Hitler sent Schaub away afterward to the Berghof to burn his private papers, which he did. Schaub survived the war and also avoided capture by the Red Army. *HHA*

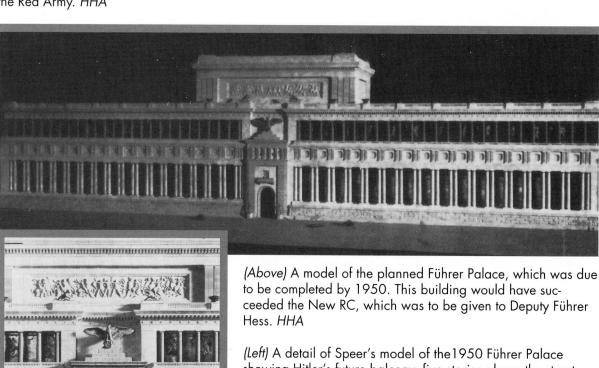

(Above) A model of the planned Führer Palace, which was due to be completed by 1950. This building would have succeeded the New RC, which was to be given to Deputy Führer Hess. *HHA*

(Left) A detail of Speer's model of the 1950 Führer Palace showing Hitler's future balcony, five stories above the street. The building was to occupy twenty-two million square feet. *HHA*

6 SPECIAL TRAIN *AMERIKA*, KASINO HOTEL IN ZOPPOT, AND AN OVERVIEW OF HITLER'S WAR HEADQUARTERS, 1939–1945

The Führer began World War II at the New Reich Chancellery in Berlin. Then he left for the Polish front aboard his special train, *Amerika*, where he observed—but did not direct—the initial campaign of the German Armed Forces against an active enemy in the field. He then relocated to the Kasino Hotel at Zoppot until the fall of Warsaw, after which he returned to Berlin late that month.

This chapter discusses the evolution of the early Führer Headquarters, their actual uses, the four basic building designs, and who occupied them. It provides a brief overview of all the FHQs through the end of the war as well as a short review of the various trains the German High Command used during 1939–45.

Hitler's View of OKW (High Command of the Armed Forces) and What It Entailed

As Franz W. Seidler and Dieter Zeigert noted in *Hitler's Secret Headquarters*, on one occasion Hitler told Schmundt, "I intend to make it quite clear that the Commander alone carries the responsibility and has the power of decision. The staff are his specially trained experts—no more!"

The FHQs were not only command centers, but specific personnel traveled to them with Hitler or were more permanently attached to the FHQ: Keitel (and two adjutants) as commander in chief of OKW; Jodl (and a single general staff officer) as commander in chief of Armed Forces Command Staff; Schmundt as Senior Armed Forces Führer's aide-de-camp; and Engel, von Below, and von Puttkamer as the adjutants from the three individual armed services. The latter three adjutants, along with Dr. Todt, sought and selected all the various FHQ locations, which were subject to the Führer's approval.

In addition, there was one liaison officer from each of the three arms of service assigned to the FHQ, as well as Bodenschatz from Göring, SS Gen. Karl Wolff and then General Fegelein from RFSS Himmler, Brückner from the SA, Dr. Lammers from the head office of the Nazi Party, the Reich press chief Dr. Dietrich (or his deputy, Heinz Lorenz), Ambassador Walter Hewel from the For-

eign Ministry, and a pair of physicians (SS Dr. Karl Brandt and Dr. Theodor Morell). Later Army Doctors Erwin Giesing and Hans-Karl von Hasselbach, plus SS Dr. Ludwig Stumpfegger, joined the staff.

Finally, the staff included Professor Hoffmann as the Reich's official photographer; Chief Johann (Hans) Rattenhuber, the commandant of the Reich Security Service (RSD) SS Escort Commando; and the FHQ military commandant with a security company, signals troop, motorized antiaircraft battery, and two railway antiaircraft cars. Initially—in Czechoslovakia and then Poland—this was Gen. Erwin Rommel, followed later by several others: Maj. Gen. Kurt Thomas, Lt. Col. Gustav Streve, Maj. Gen. Otto Ernst Remer, Streve (a second term), and SS man Franz Schadle.

Not listed formally, but present always nonetheless, was the Luftwaffe's motion picture and still photographer Walter Frentz, whose work appeared in the weekly German newsreels and—since the 1990s—in still format in several books and magazines.

Seidler and Ziegert noted in *Hitler's Secret Headquarters*, "The idea that Hitler might occupy a headquarters near the battle lines in the event of war was first expressed in 1938 when Col. Walter Warlimont, Head of the WFSt Land Defense Section (L), spoke of a mobile camp, but it was not until July 1942 that the term Führerhauptquartier (FHQ) was first defined in writing." Indeed, Schmundt wrote, "On grounds of secrecy, the term 'Führerhauptquartier' should only be used if there is no other way to describe what is meant."

In his work *Inside Hitler's Headquarters*, Warlimont concluded that "the term FHQ and its telephone/telex address cover name meant Hitler, his inner circle, and the WFSt field staff attached quasi-officially to the headquarters."

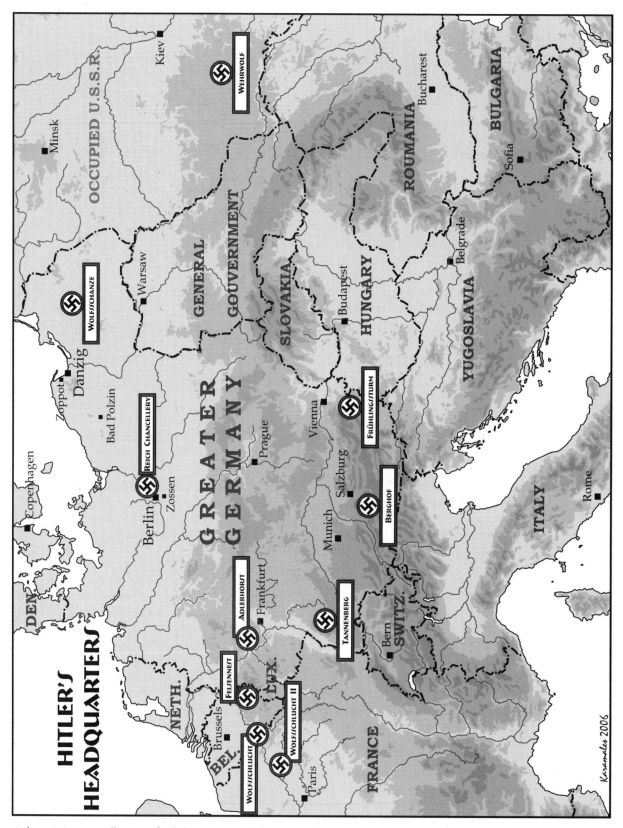

(Above) An overall map of all the wartime Führer Headquarters (FHQs) spread across Nazi Germany-occupied Europe, from as far west as Soissons in France to Vinnitsa in the Ukraine in the east. They were built, used, or planned right up until the last day of the war. *Map by Jay Karamales. © Potomac Books, Inc.*

The Track of the Wolf

Hitler used the alias "Herr Wolf" in the early days of his political career. He later gave several of his FHQs code names that included the word *wolf*: Wolfsschlucht (Wolf's Glen), Wolfsschanze (Wolf's Lair), and Werwolf (Armed Wolf).

The Führer regarded himself as a kind of predatory wolf among other political beasts, "seizing his prey from the servile herd," as he noted in statements between 1941 and 1944 in *Hitler's Table Talk*. Some of his early derivative nicknames included *Wolfschen*, or "little wolf."

The Four Basic FHQ Building Designs of the Organization Todt (OT), 1940–45

In all, nineteen FHQs were either built or under construction by the end of World War II in May 1945. There were four basic designs.

The first design consisted of bunkers either entirely above or partially below ground with fortified entrances to protect the occupants against enemy air assault. Later on during the conflict, this format also had an underground gallery.

The second design used houses that from the outside looked like German alpine chalets. They had underground bunkers that served as both living and working quarters for their residents.

The third was, according to Seidler and Ziegert in *Hitler's Secret Headquarters*, "single-story, prefabricated, barracks-type housing almost exclusively without a cellar, prepared logs being delivered for assembly on a concrete foundation. One advantage of these huts was the facility with which they could be dismantled and erected elsewhere."

Finally, the fourth design had six different sizes of wooden barracks inside a 30- to 60-centimeter thick (11.81 to 23.62 inches) concrete outer hull. These barracks were "within 10–30cm [3.94 to 11.81 inches] of the walls and [had] a concrete ceiling," added Seidler and Ziegert. "Steel plates 4cm thick could be bolted over the windows for splinter protection. The entrances were generally between 1.8 and 2.5 meters high, with two winged doors of 2cm thick steel." The foundations were laid exclusively by the Organization Todt (OT) for this type of barracks, while trains delivered the different sectional pieces, all of which could then be constructed on-site by unskilled labor, making the barracks ideal for their purposes.

The OT was also in charge of erecting car garages, flak artillery locations, sentry houses, and entrenchments and also for setting up barbed wire and additional security systems on all FHQ sites throughout the war. Indeed, following the explosion of the bomb meant to kill him at Wolfsschanze on July 20, 1944, Hitler at first believed that it had been planted by a foreign forced laborer working for the OT rather than one by of his own Army officers.

What Actually Happened at the Twice-Daily FHQ Military Situation Conferences

At noon and then again at midnight (the times varied), Hitler was comprehensively briefed by his inner-circle staffers and sometimes by outside commanders from the fighting fronts on the military events of the past twelve hours. He alone would sit at the conference table, unless Göring was also present, while the rest of the conference attendees stood around the map table.

This procedure, which Hitler began in 1940, remained substantially unchanged until the end of the war. It was a far cry from how the German Supreme Command of 1914–18 treated its so-called Supreme Warlord, Kaiser Wilhelm II, who was only informed and never consulted beforehand of decisions his supposed subordinate commanders had already made. Hitler led the war effort from May 1940 onward, rather than cede control.

Hitler's Wartime Military FHQs, 1939–45

The Polish Campaign of 1939

Hitler began the war from the New Reich Chancellery in Berlin on September 1, 1939. September 4–18 he went aboard *Amerika* (whose name was changed to *Brandenburg* after February 1, 1943) and traveled through eastern Germany via Bad Polzin to Gross-Born in Pomerania, then to Ilnau in upper Silesia, then to Gogolin near Oppeln, and to Goddentow near Danzig. Then he stayed at the Kasino Hotel in Zoppot, Poland during September 18–25.

The Führer used his train as a mobile headquarters for the first of two campaigns of the war, while Göring followed in his own train, and von Ribbentrop and Himmler traveled together in that of the Foreign Office. Hitler took daily car trips from *Amerika* to visit the front and then returned each night.

Zoppot was a pleasant seaside resort for bathers, and Hitler stayed in room numbers 251–253 of the Kasino Hotel on Nordstrasse, on the Bay of Danzig. There he received an imperial Japanese delegation headed by the Army's Field Marshal Count Hisaichi Terauchi and the Navy's Adm. Osumi Mineo on September 20.

The next day, Hitler took a boat ride to inspect the German Navy battleship *Schleswig-Holstein* that had begun the war at Danzig by blasting the Polish coastal fortress of Westerplatte. Hitler's RSD protective force was housed at the Victoria Hotel nearby.

On September 26, the Führer returned to the New RC in Berlin. From September 27, 1939, to May 9, 1940, the

FHQ was located at the Berghof on the Obersalzberg, in conjunction with the second Reich Chancellery at Bischofswiesen, both in southern Germany. During this time, Hitler made some trips to FHQ New RC in Berlin and elsewhere to plan the campaigns in both Denmark and Norway in April–June 1940.

The 1940 Western Campaign in Belgium, Holland, Luxembourg, and France

The campaign opened May 10, 1940. For forty-three days, Hitler stayed at FHQ Felsennest (Rocky Nest or Eyrie) at Rodert, Münsterefiel; from June 6 to June 25, he moved to FHQ Wolfsschlucht I at Brûly-de-Pesche, Belgium; and from June 26 to July 6, he moved to FHQ Tannenberg (Pine Mountain) at Kniebis in western Germany's famous Black Forest. Hitler returned to Berlin after the campaign was won, and for much of the rest of the year, Hitler stayed at FHQ Berghof.

The Greek and Yugoslavian Campaigns, Operation Barbarossa, and North Africa, 1941

The Führer began the new year at FHQ Berghof—January 1–27 and February 7–March 14—and spent the rest of the month at FHQ New RC Berlin. He passed the Balkan campaign—code-named Fruhlingsturm (Spring Storm)—aboard *Amerika*, parked on a remote track at the small village railway station of Monichkirchen, Austria, 35 kilometers (56.33 miles) south of Wiener Neustadt (Vienna New City) from April 11 to April 26.

As with the 1939 Polish campaign, Hitler's *Amerika* served as his FHQ for the campaigns in Greece and Yugoslavia. The train was generally stationary—steam up at all times—near the entrance of a protective tunnel in case of enemy air raids, and the special trains for Göring, Himmler, von Ribbentrop, and the Army High Command were all in the same general area as well. Operation Spring Storm staff members were located at Innsbruck, while OKH was located at the Weiner Neustadt Military Academy.

Although Hitler would use *Amerika* many more times over the war years to travel back and forth from his FHQs to Berlin and Munich, it never saw any further service as an active campaign headquarters.

In May 1945, all German High Command special trains—most of them fully intact—were captured by the Allies. Many continued in service until well into the 1970s for both Allied and, later, West German government officials.

With the Balkan campaign won, Hitler returned to FHQ New RC Berlin until May 9, 1941, when he moved to FHQ Berghof until June 11. Then he returned to Berlin to prepare for the opening of the Eastern Front campaign against the Soviet Union.

The Führer expected that Operation Barbarossa would be over in four weeks; it lasted four years instead. He spent from June 24 to August 27 at FHQ Wolfsschanze in Rastenburg, East Prussia, Germany (today Ketrzyn, Poland).

Hitler spent the night of August 27–28 with Mussolini at FHQ Askania South at Krosno, Poland, and was back at Wolfsschanze during August 28–December 31. He had a brief stopover at Berlin's Reichstag on December 11 to declare war on the United States of America—the only country with which he did so.

The Second Year of the North African and Russian Campaigns, 1942

The Führer stayed at FHQ Wolfsschanze during January 1–June 11, 1942. He then went to FHQ Berghof June 11–20, returning to FHQ Wolfsschanze for June 20–July 15. During July 16–October 31, the Führer's headquarters was Werwolf, located on former Soviet soil in the Ukraine at Vinnitsa. Then he moved back to FHQ Wolfsschanze for November 1–5. He also attended diplomatic meetings at FHQ Castle Klessheim in Salzburg, Austria.

For November 7–11, he was at FHQ Führerbau in Munich and FHQ New RC in Berlin, then at FHQ Berghof during November 12–22. He returned to FHQ Wolfsschanze from November 23 to December 31 for the opening phase of the siege of Stalingrad.

The 1943 Campaigns of Russia, North Africa, Sicily, and Italy

For the rest of the Battle of Stalingrad and its aftermath, Hitler stayed first at FHQ Wolfsschanze from January 1 to February 18. He then went to FHQ Werwolf during February 18–March 13, returning to FHQ Wolfsschanze during March 13–21. From March 22 to May 2, the Führer stayed at FHQ Berghof and planned the Kursk offensive in the Soviet Union from there. He visited FHQ New RC Berlin, then returned to FHQ Berghof during May 21–June 30.

During Kursk, he returned to FHQ Wolfsschanze to conduct that battle while overcoming the fall of the Duce in Italy. He went to FHQ Werwolf for the third and final time on August 27 for only a single day. He returned to FHQ Wolfsschanze through November 7. During November 8–15, Hitler was once again at FHQ Berghof, and then went back to FHQ Wolfsschanze for November 16 through December 3. By then, the Allies had taken both North Africa and Sicily.

The D-Day Landings in Normandy and the Ongoing Russian Campaign, 1944

From January 1 until February 23, 1944, the Führer remained at FHQ Wolfsschanze. He then left for FHQ Berghof during February 24–June 16, where he confronted the Allied D-Day invasion (he was at both FHQ Berghof and FHQ Castle Klessheim on June 6). He attended a one-day meeting with Field Marshals Gerd von Rundstedt and Erwin Rommel at FHQ Wolfsschlucht 2 at Margival, France, on June 17 before returning to FHQ Berghof again from June 18 until July 8.

Hitler went back to FHQ Wolfsschanze in East Prussia for one day—July 9—then returned to FHQ Berghof for his final stay July 10–14. Hitler possibly suspected that he would never see his beloved Bavaria again. He didn't.

Four days after his return to FHQ Wolfsschanze, the Army Bomb Plot of July 20 nearly killed him. However, the Führer stayed on until he left Rastenburg and East Prussia for good on November 20, bound for Berlin.

Back in FHQ New RC Berlin from November 20 until December 9, the wounded and ill Führer had a crucial operation on his vocal chords on November 22. He also prepared the last great German offensive of the war, the Battle of the Bulge, and actually waged it from FHQ Adlerhorst (Eagle's Eyrie) at Ziegenberg near Bad Nauheim, Germany, during December 10–31.

The 1945 Battles for Eastern Europe, Austria, and Germany

The year 1945 opened with the Führer at FHQ Adlerhorst until January 15. Then he used *Brandenburg* for the last time, leaving the Western Front for Berlin at 6:00 PM and arriving in the capital the next morning at 10:00 AM.

German Army engineers in Bavaria blew up Hitler's personal coach before the U.S. Army captured the rest of the train in the spring of 1945. The remaining original coaches were returned to the West German government a decade later.

The last coach to remain in service with the Bundesbahn—dining car #10245 (renumbered 8840227)—was scrapped in 1973. At that time, however, sleeping car #10222 (renumbered 8940322) was still used by the president of the Federal Republic of Germany. Göring's own personal car also survived the war.

Hitler stayed at FHQ New RC Berlin for the final time January 16–February 15. He retreated to the underground FHQ Führer-bunker for the final period of the war, from February 15 until April 30, on which date he and Eva Braun-Hitler committed suicide.

(Left) On the balcony of the Hotel Imperial in Vienna in April 1938, from left to right are: Frick, Hitler, and Himmler. *HHA*

(Above) Hitler traveling by rail in his private coach in a Reichsbahn (National Railroad) train before the war, as seen in this previously unpublished view. HHA

(Above) A German Army sentry walks his post while the Führer's *Amerika* sits parked at the Austrian railway station at Monichkirchen outside Vienna during the ten-day-long Balkan campaign of April 1941. HHA

(Below) The Führer strolls next to *Amerika* in April 1941 with his Luftwaffe adjutant—Colonel von Below—at Monichkirchen, Austria, sometime during the German campaigns in Greece and Yugoslavia. Note the German Reichsbahn eagle and letters emblazoned on the side of the coach. HHA

(Below Right) The Führer greets a happy German throng during one of his many peacetime cross-country journeys by rail. Of the four modes of transportation available to him, he preferred them in this order: road, rail, air, and water. HHA

(Left) The future "Desert Fox," Erwin Rommel (left), sharing a laugh with RFSS Himmler (right) aboard Hitler's train in Czechoslovakia on March 15, 1939. *HHA*

(Middle left) One of the Führer's military situation conferences aboard *Amerika* during the Polish campaign of September 1939. From left to right are: Göring, Bodenschatz, Jodl (obscured in background), Keitel, Army adjutant Capt. Gerhard Engel, Hitler, and von Ribbentrop. *HHA*

(Below) Reichsführer SS Himmler arrives at Hitler's train for a conference on a rainy day at Mönichkirchen, Austria, during the Balkan campaign in April 1941. Seen here from left to right are: a saluting Reichsbahn official, Hitler in rain cape, Schaub, Brückner (obscured), Himmler, and an RSD man running behind him on the wooden platform. *HHA*

(Right) This previously unpublished photo is of the Duce's visit to Göring's Luftwaffe headquarters—code-named Robinson—at the former imperial hunting lodge of Kaiser Wilhelm II at Rominten, East Prussia, on August 26, 1941. Sitting down to a luncheon next to Göring's own special train, *Asien* (Asia), are, from left to right: Göring, unknown Luftwaffe officer (standing), Mussolini—looking at a special commemorative photo album of his late son, Bruno, who was a pilot in the Italian Regia Aeronautica (Royal Air Force), and had died in an airplane accident shortly before—and Hitler. The other two men (backs to camera) are unknown. Göring's train, just as Hitler's, survived the end of the war. *HGA*

(Left) The luncheon over, the official party departs from the wooden platform to inspect the field headquarters of Reich Marshal Göring. From left to right are: Mussolini, Italian Army Marshal Ugo Cavallero, Göring, Keitel, Schmundt, and Hitler. Behind them on the platform are an unknown Luftwaffe officer (left) and Schaub (right). *HGA*

(Left) Göring (left, in white shirt and leather hunting jacket) meets in the conference coach aboard *Asien* in this previously unpublished view of June 19, 1940, during a work session at Ivoir, France. *HGA*

(Below) The seaside resort of Zoppot in 1939 when Hitler had a temporary FHQ located there. The Kasino Hotel is at the base of the pier, to the left. *DSG*

(Top) A good view of the Kasino Hotel at Zoppot in 1943. *DSG*

(Above) The Führer and his immediate staff emerge from one of the buildings on the grounds of FHQ Zoppot's Kasino Hotel in September 1939. From left to right are: Rommel with maps, Dr. Lammers, Hitler, Engel, Schmundt, Bodenschatz, and an unknown Army officer behind him. *HHA*

FHQ FELSENNEST, FHQ WOLFSSCHLUCHT, AND FHQ TANNENBERG, 1940

Felsennest (Rocky Nest/Crag's Nest/ Mountain Nest/Rock Eyrie/Nest of Rocks/Cliff Nest): The "Accidental" FHQ, May 10–June 6, 1940

Hitler rejected the planned Western Front FHQ Adlerhorst, a complex at Castle Ziegenberg in Germany, for many reasons, one of which was that its signal installations would not be operational until mid-June—too late for the spring 1940 campaign's opening guns. He chose instead FHQ Felsennest near Münstereifel—50 miles southwest of Cologne in the Rhineland, 45 kilometers (28 miles) from the Belgian frontier.

FHQ Felsennest was named after the 400-meter-high (437.45 yards) forested hilltop location above the German village of Rodert, near Münstereifel, 30 kilometers (18.64 miles) south of Bonn. Seidler and Ziegert stated in *Hitler's Secret Headquarters*, "The enclosure of 30 hectares boasted a bunker and anti-aircraft emplacements with barracks erected by the Organization Todt (OT)," the Nazi construction unit that built all the wartime FHQs.

Felsennest was composed of four bunkers, with 250 square meters (299 square yards) of floor space, and a pair of fortified blockhouses and a trio of barracks. This FHQ was constructed in almost eight months of ten-hour workdays by four hundred laborers.

Hitler had a modest bunker that housed an office, a bedroom, and two smaller rooms for Schaub and Linge, as well as a bathroom and a kitchen. Living in the other half were Keitel, Jodl, Schmundt, and Brandt. The bunker was air-conditioned because it had no windows, and it had such acoustics that Keitel later claimed he could hear the Führer turning newspaper pages on the bunker's other side.

There was another pair of barracks on a hill nearby, one of which had a dining hall that sat twenty, and a map of France on its windowless longer wall. Jodl's staff officer Capt. Willi Deyle and some clerks occupied the other hut. Warlimont, who was there, recalled in *Inside Hitler's Headquarters* that

a path, which lost itself in low scrub over 100 or 200 yards further on, led up from

the farmhouse through a high barbed wire fence to Hitler's quarters, HQ Area 1. Here he lived with the usual entourage of generals and aides from the Chancellery in Berlin. The concrete fortifications which served as working and living accommodations covered a wide area. Even the mess was in a pillbox. The central point, however, was a small wooden hut, no more than 9–12 feet square, up on a hill, which was the map and briefing room and in which all the more important conferences took place. Here there was a fine view over the mountains and woods of the Eifel.

Owing to the preponderance of mud, catwalks had been constructed for walking. The bunkers were air-conditioned, and the Führer's principal worry about all his FHQ sites was an Allied paradrop to capture the entire FHQ—a fear that increased the longer the war went on. Here, at Felsennest, the buildings were covered with camouflage nets and straw mats and were surrounded by a wire fence.

From this historic location, exactly one-half hour after his arrival there, Hitler launched his victorious assault on France at 5:35 AM on May 10, 1940. Later, FHQ Felsennest was considered to be the most scenically beautiful of all the wartime sites chosen. Indeed, Hitler's secretary Christa Schröder noted in her postwar memoir *Hitler Was My Boss*, "The woods, fresh with spring, were filled with birdsong . . . as his bunker was very small, he held most of his conversations in the open air."

On the military side, Hitler dealt with OKW Chief Keitel, Head of Operations Staff Jodl, and, on occasion, Jodl's deputy, Warlimont. Amazingly, the three service chiefs—von Brauchitsch, Raeder, and Göring—had no special place in the actual operational planning and, indeed, only saw the Führer from time to time when he specifically called them to a FHQ. This was a major flaw in Hitler's idiosyncratic style of running the war, it has been noted.

Both Keitel and Jodl retained their posts from the first to the last day of the war, the latter having the most influence on Hitler and the former playing a greater role than that which he has ever been credited. Keitel twice blocked von Reichenau's appointment to head the Army: in 1938, and again in 1941.

From the Polish campaign until mid-May 1940, the Führer let his generals run the war, but with the Western Front, he began to intervene for the first time, increasingly in the martial operations laid out by OKH, and especially as he gained more confidence in his own supposed skills in those areas. The hands-off policy of the former Kaiser was not for him. Until 1943, Hitler also allowed Grand Admiral Dr. Raeder to run the Navy, and Reich Marshal Göring the Luftwaffe; then he fired the one and replaced the other—in effect—with himself, a strategy that he copied from the Duce in Italy. In Russia, as in France before, Hitler practiced the policy of obtaining his industrial goals before destroying the enemy's forces, which drove his generals to distraction. All of this caused increasing problems for Halder and von Brauchitsch, as the former noted in his diary for May 17, 1940: "The Führer is terribly nervous. He is frightened by his own success, is unwilling to take any risks and is trying to hold us back." Jodl agreed in his diary: "He rages and shouts that we are going about it the right way to ruin the entire operation and are running the risk of defeat." In *Inside Hitler's Headquarters,* Warlimont called this tendency "Hitler's complete lack of balance . . . having no depth of knowledge and experience." Keitel and Jodl soothed his spirits, though, and the quartet got on with the war.

The political decision to let the British Army escape at Dunkirk so as to make the English more amenable to a peaceful, negotiated end of the war (and to realize the Luftwaffe commander in chief's desire to crush the British Expeditionary Force [BEF] with his air weapon alone) went against a tactic advocated by von Brauchitsch, Halder, and von Rundstedt: to allow the Army's advance to beat the enemy.

Instead, Hitler ordered the Army to halt, and three hundred thousand men escaped to fight another day. There was, however, a certain historical precedent for Hitler's action that is never mentioned: Imperial Chancellor Prince Otto von Bismarck's initial refusal in 1871 to allow the German Army to take Paris for fear that it would embitter the French toward another, future war, although their defeat at the hands of Prussia did anyway. A bad military decision, it was good politically, and Hitler had to consider both aspects.

On May 18, 1940, the new Italian ambassador to Berlin, Dino Alfieri, arrived at the FHQ to tell the Führer that Fascist Italy would enter the war on June 10, 1940; the two men met again on the thirtieth at the nearby Hotel Dreesen. Hitler left Felsennest for good on June 5, 1940, and went to his second French campaign FHQ.

Five years later, as the U.S. Army drove toward the village of Rodert, German engineers blew up Felsennest's buildings on the hill above the village and also burned the wooden structures. Today, it is difficult to locate the former FHQ without a military survey map because even the road that led to it was dug up in 1974.

Wolfsschlucht (Wolf's Gorge/Wolf's Glen): The Belgian FHQ at Brûly-de-Pesche, June 6–25, 1940

The rapid German Army advance led Hitler to move into conquered Belgium to a site closer to the Western Front in the tiny fishing village of Brûly-de-Pesche—9 kilometers (5.59 miles) northwest of Rocroi and south of Philippeville—on the French border. Originally codenamed Waldwiese (Forest Meadow), the second 1940 FHQ was renamed Wolfsschlucht (Wolf's Gorge or Wolf's Glen), and Hitler remained there June 6–25, 1940.

Hitler did not like the location because his bunker was situated in thick brushwood and bugs plagued the buildings. There were no human inhabitants, however, as they had all been evacuated prior to his arrival. Although the cement of the bunker was not yet dry, there was a small fountain and even a special garden with gravel walking paths laid out for him. The Führer lived in a small hut instead of the bunker, while his working staff was housed in the village school and church.

Warlimont recalled in *Inside Hitler's Headquarters,* "The map room was in the local school. Our . . . offices were in wooden huts, but living accommodations were in a country house nearby, since the village itself was occupied by Hitler's immediate entourage. OKH was located some miles away in the neighborhood of Chimay," in which twenty-five houses were specially prepared for that use.

Hitler's personal protection in the area was ensured by jailing local civilian hostages in nearby Dinant prison. There was also a makeshift grass airfield beside the commandant's building on the village's southern end. In all, Brûly-de-Pesche had but ten farmhouses plus the church and school. The closest real airfield was a few kilometers away at Gros-Caillou.

As before at Felsennest, the Führer spent as much time as possible outside, especially since the varnish inside the buildings caused his eyes to swell up. He felt insecure at Brûly as well. Hitler never even used his own bunker, though the RAF routinely flew over the village and once dropped some incendiary bombs that hit the barracks of his SS and RSD guard units.

Meanwhile, General Halder was angry that the drive took twenty minutes by road from OKH to FHQ, and von Brauchitsch—the commander in chief of the Army—only attended Wolfsschlucht briefings twice!

As the second phase of the French campaign got under way on June 5, 1940, the Germans approved another FQH site—Wolfsschlucht 2 (W2)—to allow the Führer to be closer to the action in the field. Hitler never occupied it that year, however, because France sued for peace first.

Brûly-de-Pesche was the site of the famous occasion when Hitler stamped his right foot down on the ground in joy when he heard that the French were giving up, an incident captured forever in Walter Frentz's famous newsreel. The village's own St. Mary's church was where the armistice terms were drawn up on June 21, 1940. They were signed by both the French and German delegations the next day at Compiègne, where the Germans had surrendered on November 11, 1918.

An extremely rare picture of Hitler and RAD women at FHQ Tannenberg, 1940. *Frentz*

With the Battle of France over, Göring began his aerial Battle of Britain, but after its failure, Hitler postponed Operation Sea Lion, the planned invasion of the British Isles on October 12, 1940. Four years later, the English Channel was duly crossed, but by the Allies, not the Germans.

In 1970, Speer recalled in *Inside the Third Reich* the following telling anecdote of the Führer's stay at Wolfsschlucht in 1940, after the victorious French campaign:

> **Hitler was pacing back and forth on the gravel path in front of his house. . . . I heard a snatch of the conversation: "Now we have shown what we are capable of," Hitler was saying. "Believe me, Keitel, a campaign against Russia would be like a child's game in a sandbox by comparison." In radiant good humor, he bade me goodbye. . . .**

Tannenberg (Pine Mountain): Hitler's Third and Last Western Campaign FHQ, June 28–July 5, 1940

The location of Hitler's third and final Western Front FHQ during the period of June 28 (some accounts say June 27) through July 5, 1940, was code-named Tannenberg, possibly after von Hindenburg's August 1914 victory over the Imperial Russian Army in East Prussia. FHQ Tannenberg was built in the winter of 1939–40 on Mt. Kniebis in the dense, northern Black Forest of Germany.

Hitler arrived at Tannenberg at 11:00 AM on June 28, 1940. The facility had the usual bunkers, wooden barracks, and blockhouses, with Hitler's personal suite located in the nearby inns. His own bunker was partially buried in the earth, while dense woods and barbed wire fencing encircled the overall compound. There was also a small landing strip for courier aircraft.

While OKH moved to the former Fontainbleau of Emperor Napoleon I, the Führer opted instead for a sort of short vacation to visit the captured Maginot Line forts and his own former battlefields of World War I.

On July 1, 1940, Hitler and Dr. Göbbels met again with Italian ambassador Alfieri to plan his triumphant return to the German capital. On that day he also received a delegation of female RAD (German Labor Service) members, the only women other than his four secretaries and two cooks to be present at any field FHQs. Hitler also received the draft of the projected Operation Sea Lion from Jodl and Warlimont, the invasion of the British Isles that never materialized.

The Führer was upset when he learned that he would be directing Sea Lion from the projected Ziegenberg-based FHQ, which he had rejected for the 1940 campaign in the west as too opulent for his common tastes. His final days at Tannenberg were spent drafting his upcoming victory "peace-with-Britain speech." He boarded *Amerika* at 1:00 PM on July 5, bound for Berlin. He never saw FHQ Tannenberg again. On July 6, the Führer returned to Berlin, having been away from his capital for almost two full months, his longest absence since taking office in 1933. He gave the speech before the Reichstag in Berlin on July 19, 1940, but it failed to induce the British to end the fighting.

In preparation for launching Sea Lion, the Führer's bodyguard squads left Tannenberg and moved to FHQ Adlerhorst at Castle Ziegenberg. A small guard unit stayed in the compound, but the Tannenberg FHQ was never utilized again. In the summer of 1944, Jodl raised the possibility of using Tannenberg again as a field FHQ, but the idea never came to fruition.

In 1945 U.S. Army engineers demolished it to deny future tourists an attraction. Another version says the Germans destroyed it, and a third claims the First French Army destroyed it after its capture.

(Above) Von Below and Hitler exit from the Führer's underground bunker at FHQ Felsennest, with the thrown-back, screened-in entrance as conceal-ment from both the air and the ground. *HHA*

(Left) A good aerial view of the German village of Rodert, as seen from atop the wooded hill at FHQ Felsennest, just across the German-Belgian frontier that was invaded on May 10, 1940. Warlimont's Section L (National Defense Branch), the most important grouping within the Armed Forces Leadership Staff, was housed in the village. *HHA*

(Right) A famous group photo of all Hitler's Nazi "band of brothers" in the military-political inner circle at FHQ Felsennest. From left to right, first row: Bruckner, Dr. Dietrich, Keitel, Hitler, Jodl, Martin Bormann, von Below, and Hoffmann. Second row: Engel, Dr. Brandt, von Puttkamer, Lorenz, Bodenschatz (in front of Lorenz), Hewel, unknown Army officer, Schaub (behind Jodl's cap), Wunsche (behind Schaub), Wolff, Dr. Morell, and Schultze. *HHA*

(Above) A surprised German Army sentry (left) reacts as the Führer and his entourage descend the hill from FHQ Felsennest above and head toward the village of Rodert, Germany. From left to right are: Schulze, Engel, unknown man, Bruckner, Hitler giving a casual Nazi salute, von Below, and Schmundt. *HHA*

(Right) A good Luftwaffe aerial reconnaissance photo showing the camouflaged Führerbunker atop the wooded hill at FHQ Felsennest, with the figures at lower left providing both scope and size. Note, too, the small building at upper right. *HHA*

(Above) A closer view of the same structure from a different angle. *HHA*

(Below) A side view of the map bunker, showing the camouflaged netting at right. *HHA*

(Above) A still closer view of the same building, showing the patio (above) and entrance at the bottom of the steps (right), with the concealing camouflage screen in place at left. From mid-May 1940, Hitler was either ordering or being consulted on all military decisions. On May 24, 1940, he ordered German armor and infantry to halt outside the port of Dunkirk, France, and thus allowed the trapped men of the BEF to escape by sea to England. *HHA*

Three views of Hitler's personal combined workroom and bedroom at FHQ Felsennest. *HHA*

(Above) The front view of the camouflage netting covering one of the compound's log cabins. *HHA*

(Above) A previously unpublished view from under similar netting, showing, from left to right: Schmundt, SS General Wolff, and von Ribbentrop. *JRA*

(Left) Exit Hitler, stage left, from one of the camouflaged bunkers. Stated Toland in *Adolf Hitler*, "Hitler left *Felsennest* on the eve of the fall of Dunkirk with instructions to preserve the entire area as a 'national monument.' Every room in the complex was to be kept intact, every nameplate to remain on its door." *HHA*

(Right) Underneath the netting in this previously unpublished view are Keitel (left) and von Ribbentrop. In January 1941, the entire FHQ was taken over by the Nazi Party (Hess) to become a national tourist attraction after the Third Reich won the war. Countered Warlimont in *Inside Hitler's Headquarters,* "Hitler's preservation order did not cover the OKH 'hunting lodge,' although they had—in fact—been the architects of the victory," and *not* Hitler. *JRA*

(Below) The interior of the map study in the OKW barracks' situation room. Hitler's desire that FHQ Felsennest become a postwar Nazi theme park was thwarted in 1945 when it was blown up by the retreating German Army in face of the advancing V Corps of the U.S. Third Army. *HHA*

(Above) FHQ Felsennest.
From left to right in the
map room are: Capt.
Willi Deyle, Jodl, Hitler
and Keitel (obscured),
1940. *Walter Frentz*

(Left) A photo of the
map room taken through
the open windows,
revealing, from left to
right: Hitler, Deyle, and
Keitel, pointing out a
map feature. Only ruins
exist today. *HHA*

(Top) According to the Hoffmann photo studio website, the Führer spent the night of June 1–2, 1940, at FHQ Schloss Annapes. *HHA*

(Above) From left to right are Keitel, Schaub, Hitler, Bodenschatz, and Brückner at Schloss Annapes. *HHA*

(Right) The service chiefs at FHQ Wolfsschlucht in 1940. In this previously unpublished photograph, from left to right are: von Brauchitsch (Army), an RSD guard, Keitel (OKW), Hitler, and Raeder (Navy) in forward stride. *HHA*

(Above) The only known photo of OT workers laying the foundation for an eventual Führerbunker at FHQ Wolfsschlucht. Hitler never used the bunker. *HHA*

(Left) A good aerial view of Brûly-de-Pesche. The OT took the spire off the church steeple at lower right, hoping the absent church spire would help disguise the site from the RAF. The wooded area in the upper right corner contained both the concrete bunker and the wooden chalet. Staff officers used the dark building at center, while the white house served as a casino and officers' mess. The grave of SS man Hans Bastians was to the left of the Wolf's Palace Kasino, and the field above (left) was where the Fieseler Storch courier planes landed and took off. It was hoped Keitel got the vicarage. After the Führer left Brûly-de-Pesche for FHQ Tannenberg, his chalet was torn down on June 26, 1940. *HHA*

(Left) Hitler's unused bunker at FHQ Wolfsschlucht in 1940. This FHQ was initially code-named Anlage Waldwiese (Camp Forest Meadow) but was changed to FHQ Wolfsschlucht by Hitler, reflecting his former alias as Herr Wolf during the early years of the Nazi Party. After the war, the bunker was owned by the Count of Ouitremont and was then the only surviving structure at any of Hitler's former wartime headquarters. The Wolfpalast (Wolf's Palace Kasino) was the former Brûly-de-Pesche village inn that was taken over as a residence by the FHQ staff. The OKH headquarters was situated at Forges, a small village just south of Chimay, Belgium, about ten miles northwest of Brûly-de-Pesche. Note the white painted rings around the tree trunks, which served as nighttime blackout walking guides at eye level. *HHA*

Two previously unpublished views of Hitler's wooden chalet at Brûly-de-Pesche. This chalet was Hitler's real residence while at FHQ Wolfsschlucht. Near his bunker was the Kasino, as well as a few other lightly built structures, in the small wood to the west of Brûly. As with all other past and future FHQs—except New RC Berlin—the compound was surrounded by a barbed wire fence. The first photo shows the front porch of Hitler's chalet, while the second shows von Ribbentrop and Hitler walking toward it from the side. Note, too, the painted tree trunks. *HHA and JRA*

(Above) A previously unpublished "telephone photo opportunity," beloved of all press agents every-where! This shot looks into the open window of the Brûly-de-Pesche FHQ map room, as Keitel (right) looks over a map. On June 12, 1940, a search team found a suitable site for yet another Western Front FHQ that was never used: at the south end of a railroad tunnel at Rilly Germaine, south of Reims, France. The French declared Paris an open city on June 14, 1940. *HHA*

(Above) At work in the map room with, from left to right, are: Keitel, Diehl, Jodl, Hitler, and von Brauchitsch. Hitler is about to take the pencil from von Brauchitsch's hand, as seen in a famous Walter Frentz newsreel sequence that is still shown on worldwide television to this day. *HHA*

(Left) Hitler alone sat while all of his subordinates stood, Hitler's trick of maintaining control over his many paladins. From left to right are: Dr. Brandt, Wolff, Dr. Morell, unknown aide, Engel, Bodenschatz, Martin Bormann, Dr. Dietrich, Keitel, and (with back to camera) Jodl, all at FHQ Wolfsschlucht. On June 21, 1940, the Führer was driven to the forest of Compiègne, France, to receive the defeated French delegates in the same railroad dining car the French used on November 11, 1918, thus standing recent modern history on its head. *HHA*

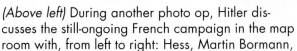

(*Above left*) During another photo op, Hitler discusses the still-ongoing French campaign in the map room with, from left to right: Hess, Martin Bormann, Keitel, an unknown officer, Wolff, and Wünsche. The Führer departed Brûly-de-Pesche on June 23, 1940, to fly to Paris for a scant few hours—his only trip there—and then spent the next two days visiting his old World War I battlefields with two unit veterans of that time. He left Brûly-de-Pesche for the last time on June 28, 1940, bound for FHQ Tannenberg. *HHA*

(*Above right*) A famous shot of Hitler using a pencil and magnifying glass to mark the map in the same sequence of map room photos with Bodenschatz at center and Wolff at right. *HHA*

(*Left*) On the evening of June 25, 1940, Hitler waited at FHQ Wolfsschlucht for the sound of a German Army soldier's bugle at 1:35 AM to signal that the negotiated and signed armistice with defeated France had taken effect. From left to right are: an unknown man, Speer, unknown officer, Wolff, Amann, unknown man, Hitler, Diehl, Schaub, Martin Bormann, Jodl, Schmundt, Dr. Brandt, and two other unknown officers. (In the next photo [previously unpublished], the same group has risen to its feet.) Speer recalled in *Inside the Third Reich*, "That night we sat with Hitler around a deal table in the simple room of a peasant house. Shortly after the agreed time, Hitler gave orders to turn out the light and open the windows. Silently, we sat in the darkness, swept by the sense of experiencing a historic moment so close to the author of it. Outside, a bugler blew the traditional signal for the end of fighting. . . . Someone, overcome by emotion, blew his nose. Then Hitler's voice sounded, soft and unemphatic: 'This responsibility . . .' and a few moments later, 'Now switch the light on.' The trivial conversation continued, but for me it remained a rare event. I thought I had for once seen Hitler as a human being." *HHA*

(Left) The historic scene concluded, the entire company rises with Hitler and all give the Nazi salute—even the usually nonpolitical military service officers, such as von Puttkamer (dark uniform, third from right) and von Below (far right). *HHA*

(Below left) The lonely grave of SS Lt. Hans Bastians at Brûly-de-Pesche, as seen in this previously unpublished photograph. He was Himmler's personal driver, who had brought the RFSS to the FHQ for a conference with Hitler and who was killed by accident on June 14, 1940. While waiting for the meeting to end, Bastians's Schmiesser MP 38 machine pistol—infamously dangerous with its safety catch in the open bolt position—discharged by mistake, shooting him in the head and killing him. He was the first fatality at any FHQ location and was duly buried in the village that day with full military honors and a eulogy by his former boss, as noted in *The Hitler Book*: "He rests in German earth. This land will belong to us forever." *HHA*

(Below) A seemingly bored Hitler listens to an ebullient Himmler in the wooded area next to Hitler's chalet at Wolfsschlucht. Traces of the white painted blackout rings seen here on the trees were still visible three decades later. *HHA*

(Left) A camouflaged walkway at FHQ Wolfsschlucht in 1940. *HHA*

(Right and bottom right) Hitler waits for his Luftwaffe commander in chief, Göring, to deplane from a Fieseler Storch courier plane on the grassy airstrip just south of the Wolf's Palace Kasino at Brûly-de-Pesche on June 14, 1940, the day the French declared Paris an open city. In the second photo, Göring has deplaned and shakes hands with Hitler as Martin Bormann looks on at center. It was also at FHQ Wolfsschlucht that Hitler told his architects he wanted all his colossal building plans for Berlin and elsewhere completed by 1950, the year by which he felt Nazi Germany win the war. Wünsche stands at the far left. *HGA*

(Left) The same group proceeds from the landing strip past St. Mary's Church through the village square on June 14, 1940, at the very peak of their power. From left to right are: Hitler, Bodenschatz, Göring, an RSD man, Martin Bormann, and saluting RSD men at far right. *HGA*

(Below) On June 14, 1940, in one of the most famous German newsreel footage sequences of World War II—shot by Walter Frentz at Brûly-de-Pesche at the very moment when the Führer learned that the French had, through neutral Spanish channels, requested an armistice—Hitler raised his right foot in the air and stamped it down once onto the ground. Here, in the actual sequence of the frames as Frentz shot them, from left row top to bottom, we see this sole foot stamping. In *Adolf Hitler,* Toland called this famous incident "the jig that never was. . . . The . . . frames were cleverly 'looped' by a Canadian film expert [John Grierson], making it appear that Hitler was executing a St. Vitus–like dance." Allied propaganda officials made sure that this looped scenario was shown over and over again in both Allied and neutral country movie theaters worldwide. From left to right are: Dr. Brandt, Hewel, Hoffmann (in and out of frames), Hitler, Dr. Morell, and Wagner. *Walter Frentz*

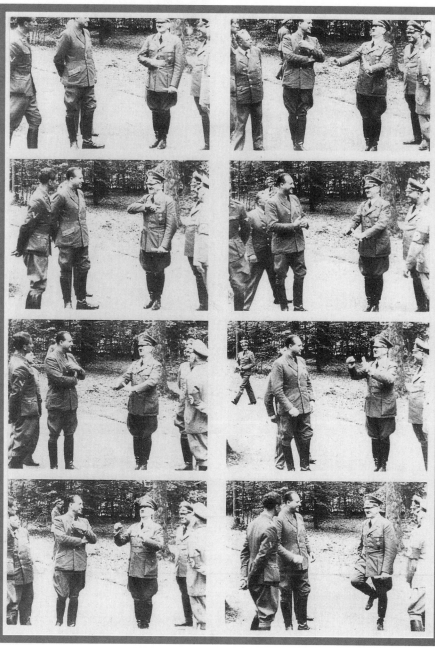

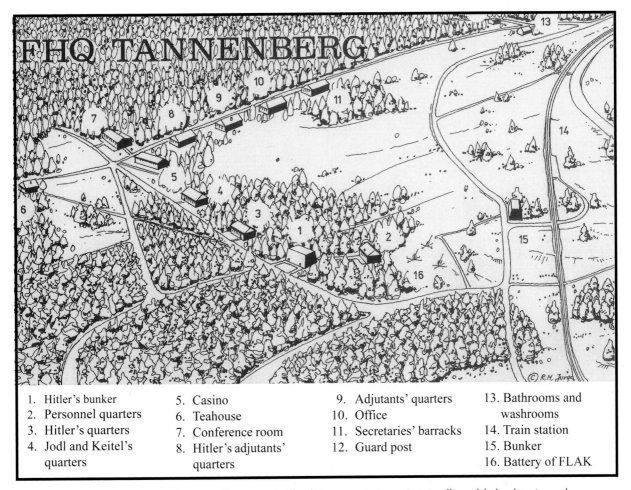

1. Hitler's bunker
2. Personnel quarters
3. Hitler's quarters
4. Jodl and Keitel's
   quarters
5. Casino
6. Teahouse
7. Conference room
8. Hitler's adjutants'
   quarters
9. Adjutants' quarters
10. Office
11. Secretaries' barracks
12. Guard post
13. Bathrooms and
    washrooms
14. Train station
15. Bunker
16. Battery of FLAK

An overview of FHQ Tannenberg in Germany's Black Forest region. *Originally published in Joseph Kaufman's* Fortress Third Reich. *Reprinted by permission of Da Capo Press/Perseus Books L.L.C.*

(Right) Author Peter Hoffmann, in *Hitler's Personal Security,* called this "*Tannenberg* FHQ, inner security perimeter, July 1940." Note the German Army sentry in the distance, with the so-called Flanders hedge (a barbed wire entanglement designed to keep out intruders) in the lower right corner of the photo. *HHA*

(Above) A working session outdoors at FHQ Tannenberg, showing—in this previously unpublished photo—from left to right: von Below, Keitel, Wünsche, Hitler, and Dr. Morell. *HHA*

(Above) A cigar-smoking RFSS Himmler (left) with Dr. Göbbels (reading a report at center) and an unknown SS aide. Steel shutters flank both the windows and doors of the building behind them. There was one bunker for Hitler, and another that served as the communications center. *HHA*

(Above left) Bruckner pets a wire-haired terrier as Himmler gestures to an unknown officer behind him in this previously unpublished photo. *HHA*

(Above right) Hitler and Hewel (right, obscured) take tea with the female RADs on the terrace of the teahouse at FHQ Tannenberg. *HHA*

(Right) A rare photo of nondancer Hitler (center), joining in with the RAD ladies in an impromptu dance routine. *HHA*

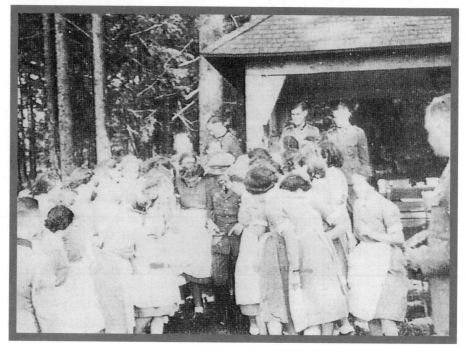

8 FHQ KLESSHEIM PALACE, 1940–1944

Castle Klessheim (also referred to as Klessheim Palace) was Hitler's Austrian State guest house outside Salzburg during 1940–44. It was used to accommodate the foreign heads of state, ministers, and military and naval officers who came there to consult with him, as on D-Day, June 6, 1944.

According to Dr. Dietrich in *Hitler*, "Klessheim Palace could be reached from Berchtesgaden in half an hour by automobile. Situated just a few miles outside Salzburg, it had been built by Fischer von Erlach as a pleasure palace for the prince-bishops of Salzburg, who had a penchant for the lighter sides of life.

With its splendid park and panoramic mountain views from its many terraces and lawns, it inspired all visitors with admiration for this beautiful part of the world. The palace had last been a possession of the House of Habsburg.... Neo-Renaissance in style, the edifice had been planned for im-

pressiveness. There was an imposing entrance drive and a grand stairway that dominated the façade.

The reception hall was located on the first floor—a huge oval-shaped room with a vaulted ceiling—and the guest rooms were actually very limited, so that only the visiting chiefs of state themselves could be housed therein. The accompanying staffs were lodged in a building away from the palace. There was also a four-leaf-clover-shaped ladies' pavilion located in a secluded spot in the park. Italian ambassador Alfieri became the first to stay at the palace.

Inside the palace itself, on the first floor, was the state suite with a salon and a bedroom, and the Duce, Gen. Ion Antonescu, Horthy, and King Boris all stayed there. Hitler and von Ribbentrop counted on these beautiful surroundings to make their visitors more conducive to the sometimes tortured logic of the daily military show briefings. Hitler preached victory even as defeat loomed ever more ominously on the horizon.

The entrance gate to the Baroque-era Klessheim Palace north of Salzburg, Austria. This was the official Reich government guest house, used mainly for Hitler's wartime meetings with foreign heads of state, diplomats, and sometimes German field marshals and generals, as in March 1944 prior to the D-Day landings. After the war, it was still used as a summit meeting site for major powers, with a hotel and restaurant owned by the local government. Today it is the Salzburg casino, complete with Nazi-era stone eagles on the front gate. *Ray and Josephine Cowdery Archive*

(Above) A view from inside the gate shot from the driveway of Klessheim Palace. Cars entered the ramp at right, with the front door at center atop it. Built between 1700 and 1709 for the city's archbishop, it was modernized by the Nazis in 1940–41 for state visitors who were going on to either FHQ Berghof or Bischofs-wiesen in Germany. Later, Hitler met with them at Klessheim as well. *Steven Lehrer*

(Left) Attending a conference at Klessheim are, from left to right: Albert Bormann, Linge, Hitler, Darges, Hewel, von Ribbentrop, and Meissner. Inside the castle's main reception hall was a huge round table with eight to ten deep armchairs. Von Manstein met there with Himmler in 1944, according to his chief wartime aide, but von Manstein never mentioned it in his postwar memoir *Lost Victories*. *HHA*

(Left) On either May 29, 1942, or April 7, 1943, Italian Army Marshal of the Empire Benito Mussolini looks doubtful (center) at this wartime military situation conference. Toland recalled in *Adolf Hitler,* "Hitler compared himself favorably with Napoleon and at the luncheon table lectured his guests for an hour and 40 minutes without interruption." Added Ciano in his diary, "Gen. Jodl—after an epic struggle—went to sleep on the divan." Here, from left to right are: Zeitzler (facing away), Dr. Schmidt, the Duce, Keitel, two unknown Italian officers, and Hitler. *HHA*

(Right) On March 17–18, 1944, are from left to right: Admiral Horthy of Hungary, unknown officer, Linge, Hitler, Albert Bormann, and another unidentified aide. After a stormy meeting in which Hitler accused the Hungarian regent of planning an Italian-style opting out of the Axis Pact (as, indeed, he was), Horthy stormed out of the hall to return home. Hitler ran after him to apologize, while von Ribbentrop staged a fake air-raid to keep Horthy's train from leaving. Upon his return to Budapest on March 19, Horthy found his country had been occupied by eleven German divisions during his absence. Thus, Hungary was kept in the war at Germany's side until the spring of 1945. *HHA*

Hitler at Castle Klessheim on D-Day, June 6, 1944. He was famously awakened late at FHQ Berghof with the news of the Allied cross-Channel invasion of Normandy from England, because Jodl felt that it was only a diversionary attack from the real invasion that was to follow elsewhere. Hitler had a show conference later that same day (seen here) at Klessheim, this time with Hungarian Gen. Dome Szotojay (seated at left). Others, from left to right, are: von Ribbentrop, Luftwaffe Chief of Staff Gen. Gunther Korten, Hitler, Warlimont, Göring, Keitel, Jodl, Hungarian Army officer, and unknown German Army officer at the far right. Hitler was rarely photographed wearing glasses, and only he and his special guest General Szotojay were seated. Hitler's rule was that he alone sat while all others stood, unless a foreign guest was present; failing that, Göring was allowed to sit as the always-ranking officer. This meeting was duly followed by other set showpieces that day, but the actual military conference had already been held before any of them. *HHA*

FHQ WOLFSSCHANZE AND NEARBY HEAD-QUARTERS OF THE STATE, PARTY, AND ARMED FORCES, 1941–1944

Hitler's main FHQ from June 1941 to late 1944 was Wolfsschanze at Rastenburg in East Prussia, which is today known as Ketrzyn, Poland. Wolfsschanze was constructed in the Rastenburg municipal forest between the towns of Partsch and Görlitz. The forest afforded excellent cover and was surrounded by both lakes and swamps. There were three approaches to the FHQ: east from Angerburg, south from the Rangsdorf airfield, and west from Rastenburg itself. The Germans initially expected to occupy FHQ Wolfsschanze for three months at most. When Maj. Otto Günsche first saw Wolfsschanze, he marveled at its size in contrast to earlier FHQs, asking Schaub if Hitler meant to spend the winter of 1941–42 there. According to *The Hitler Book*, the latter laughed and answered, "Spend the winter? What are you thinking of? We are fighting a blitzkrieg against Russia. Christmas will certainly be celebrated on the Obersalzberg, as usual!" He was wrong.

FHQ Wolfsschanze

The late Dr. Richard Raiber of Hockessin, Delaware—a well-known authority on all matters FHQ—explained the significance of the name Wolfsschanze: "Every German knows that 'Wolfsschanze' is best translated 'Wolf's Redoubt' or 'Fort Wolf,' not 'Wolf's Lair,' as it almost invariably appears in English language accounts." While I must say that I agree with Dr. Raiber, I have decided to stick with the more familiar Wolf's Lair translation because I think it would be endlessly confusing to modern readers to enact such a change now. Thus, Wolf's Lair it remains, with its far more sinister connotations.

As related by Dr. Raiber, "During the initial construction stage [summer 1940], [Wolfsschanze's] identity had been camouflaged under the code names Anlage Nord (Camp North) or Anlage N, and also Askania Chemical Works.... The Führerbunker (#11) was the principal structure in Sperrkreis [Restricted Area] 1."

Dr. Raiber also noted that the entire area

was surrounded by a fence, probably chain link topped with barbed wire, but whether it or any other fence . . . was electrified—as is

often reported—is not certain. . . . A teahouse was completed on May 27, 1942, and stood east of the Keitel Bunker (#7). Later, a new teahouse was constructed adjacent to (east of) Kasino 1 (a building that contained two dining rooms for the Führer and his inner circle), and the two came to be known as #10. It was generally in the teahouses—first the old, then the new—that Hitler sought to relax in the evenings, and these buildings were the scenes of his famous *Table Talks*.

Restricted Area 1 contained the bunkers for Hitler, Bormann, Göring, Keitel, Jodl, and Dr. Dietrich, all to the north of the railroad tracks. Entry was gained only by passage through a trio of gateways and sentry posts: east, west, and south. There were three concentric rings of security: Restricted Areas 1, 2, and 3, which were all guarded from the inside.

All of the bunkers at FHQ Wolfsschanze were either above ground (and not really bunkers in the true sense), or only partially below ground. The reason was simple: the entire area was surrounded by lakes and swamps, making for a very high water table. Thus it was impossible to build rooms far beneath the earth, as had been done in Berlin.

Overhead camouflage netting was changed seasonally, and the Germans tested the camouflage of the entire complex with aerial photography to ensure it was invisible to enemy aircraft. The netting consisted, in part, of artificial Bakelite leaves intertwined with wire. Several of the bunkers were matted with sea grass and afterward painted either green or gray for extra camouflage. Fake trees were actually placed on top of the aboveground bunkers by a Stüttgart landscaping firm that also surrounded their bases with artificial moss, as the wartime photographs clearly revealed. Camouflage netting high above the ground also concealed pathways and roads. Wilhelm Hirsch was responsible for landscaping and camouflaging all field FHQs during the war. Still, not only the Allies and the Russians, but also the Swiss Secret Service were all aware of the exact location of FHQ Wolfsschanze as of 1943.

Wolfsschanze underwent a trio of building periods: 1940–41, 1942–43, and the final phase in spring, summer, and early fall of 1944. The latter included massive reinforcement of Hitler's aboveground bunker as well as the buffing up of several others. During the 1940–41 building period, houses, barracks, and small brick-and-concrete bunkers were constructed, but they were later dwarfed by their successors. An additional ten air-raid shelters featuring six-and-a-half-foot-thick concrete shells were also built. The bedrooms were placed in these heavily protected shelters, while the workrooms were in the lighter buildings.

Bigger and better-lit additions of brick and concrete were constructed during the 1942–43 phase. They served as both living and working structures and were fitted out with windows protected by steel shutters and doorways. A large conference room was also built onto Hitler's own bunker.

In early 1944, the FHQ was moved to the Berghof on the Obersalzberg until mid-summer so that defensive upgrades could be made at FHQ Wolfsschanze. During this last construction period, all bunkers were surrounded by windowless, steel-reinforced concrete. Hitler directed that gravel fill the area in between the two concrete layers for added protection against bomb blasts. It was also during this final phase that the massive Göring Bunker and an air-raid shelter south of the road were put up. A firefighting water pool still exists a short way from the antiaircraft artillery shelter. Large chunks of steel-reinforced concrete in the water pool are from a blown-up bunker nearby, with one concrete piece weighing more than two and a half tons!

Wolfsschanze became the largest FHQ ever used, a complete town in and of itself, with two airfields, a railroad station, power and air purification facilities, a water treatment and sewer system, a large communications center, and heating system. By 1944, FHQ Wolfsschanze was home to more than two thousand people, of whom field marshals, generals, and adjutants numbered three hundred. In addition, there were 1,200 Führer Escort Battalion troops, more than 150 RSD and SS Escort Commando men, plus 300 drivers, waiters, telephone operators and typists, mechanics, barbers, and other administrative people. The occupants lived and worked inside, rarely—if ever—seeing sunlight.

The Führerbunker's rooms had ultramodern ventilation equipment, which brought in outside air via the ceiling, but the air was very humid and the ventilator noise was extremely distracting. The ventilation system also offered pressurized protection against attack by gas, plus sensors that detected gas immediately. There was only one room with natural lighting. Encased in a sturdy concrete shell in 1944, the foundation of Hitler's bunker extended almost twenty-three feet underground.

Hitler's SS aide, Otto Günsche, gave the Russians an excellent description of the expanded bunker of 1944, as reported in *The Hitler Book*:

> There was a real maze inside the bunker. From the entrance, one could reach the living rooms only through two so-called "locks" or compression chambers in the corridor . . . two antechambers that were separated from one another and from the corridor by armor-plated doors. . . . In the first corridor were the secretaries' bedrooms. . . . From the first corridor, there was a tortuous route to the second floor and the adjutants' rooms, those of Morell, Linge and the soldier-servants. From here, corridors went zigzagging towards Hitler's study and bedroom. Hitler's dining room and storeroom were also to be found in his bunker. There were pipes leading into his bedroom which could be made to discharge oxygen . . . from canisters that were kept outside the bunker in a ditch because Hitler was afraid they might blow up.

Also located in Restricted Area 1 were the RSD and SS Escort Commando troops, chauffeurs, other doctors, personal adjutants' offices, secretaries and stenographers, and the Military Personnel Office run by Schmundt. There were also a pair of air-raid bunkers, the telephone central exchange, a heating installation, the sauna, a movie theater, teahouses, and two officers' clubs.

South of the railroad tracks and the Rastenburg-Angerburg highway—and encircling Restricted Area 1—was Restricted Area 2. In the southwest part of this security ring were several brick-and-concrete one-story structures that housed FHQ military commanders and staff officers, again with officers' clubs, heating facilities, and teletype centers, and all heavily guarded. Also, as Günsche told the Russians, "In Restricted Area 2 of the HQ there was the commander of the Führer's Escort Battalion, the administration of the household, and the new railway station where three trains stood, one each for Hitler, Keitel and Warlimont—with his Wehrmacht Operations Staff."

Restricted Area 3 encircled the other two, all within the outer perimeter fencing. Located herein were machine guns and antiaircraft artillery batteries as well as an escort and armored defense battalions.

Deadly minefields and barbed wire encircled the entire Wolfsschanze compound for a spread of more than six miles. Polish removal of the minefields began in 1952 and was completed in 1955, and Polish Army engineers removed more than fifty-four thousand mines. In 1959, the Wolfsschanze site was opened as a tourist attraction and can still be visited today.

Hitler's biggest fear throughout the entire time he was in residence at Wolfsschanze was not an Allied bombing raid, but that a paratrooper operation would be mounted against it. During a daily situation conference on September 17, 1944, he asserted firmly, "(H)ere I sit, here is my entire Supreme Command, here sits the Reich Marshal, here sits the Army High Command, here sits the Reich SS Leader, here sits the Reich Foreign Minister! . . . I would not hesitate to risk two parachute divisions here, if I could capture the entire Russian leadership at one stroke" (as noted in *Hitler and His Generals: Military Conferences, 1942–45*, edited by Helmut Heiber and David M. Glantz).

Still, Hitler did nothing about it, but he needn't have worried because neither the Soviets nor the Western Allies did anything, either. While the reader may be tempted to think this oddity one of the great unsolved mysteries of World War II, he or she shouldn't. It is my opinion that nothing was done to the Nazi leadership for the very same reason that nothing was done to the Fascist Italian or the Imperial Japanese upper echelons, either: both the Allies and the Soviets held open the possibility of negotiating with the enemy at the expense of each other until the last minute, when the war was finally won.

With the Red Army but forty-three miles away at Goldap in East Prussia, Hitler left FHQ Wolfsschanze for good by special train *Brandenburg* on November 20, 1944. He arrived at the New RC two days later to have a much needed throat operation to remove a polyp from his vocal chords.

There is the possibility that Hitler was both hoping and planning on returning to FHQ Wolfsschanze someday, but this was not to be. Keitel gave orders for the implementation of Operation Inselsprung (Island Leap, or Jump), the planned destruction of not only Wolfsschanze, but also other related command centers in the region. He named Gen. Friedrich Jacob as its commander.

On January 24, 1945—while Hitler was in FHQ New RC in Berlin—the Red Army took nearby Angerburg, and Operation Inselsprung was activated. German Army engineers employed eight tons of explosives to blow up the entire FHQ complex, but even so, complete destruction was impossible, and several ruins still exist today. On January 27, 1945, the Red Army entered Rastenburg and took FHQ Wolfsschanze without a fight.

Commanding from FHQ Wolfsschanze

Hitler remained at FHQ Wolfsschanze more than 800 days, protected and served by 2,100 civilians and military

troops. From this site, Hitler made many fateful and sometimes catastrophic decisions. Speer noted in *Inside the Third Reich*, "A few trips to the front could have shown him and his staff the fundamental errors that were costing so much blood. Hitler and his military advisors thought they could lead the Army from their maps. . . . Hitler overestimated the merits of the telephone, radio, and teletype, for thanks to this apparatus, the responsible army commanders were robbed of every chance for independent action, in contrast to earlier wars. Hitler was constantly intervening on their sectors of the front." To this assessment, Warlimont added his own in *Inside Hitler's Headquarters*: "The basic fault in Hitler's leadership was the desire to command in detail without having studied the background adequately."

Hitler lived, slept, and worked in his bunker, rising late, eating breakfast by himself, and reading situation reports from both the fighting fronts and the bombed-out cities of the Third Reich. The solitary Führer took a one-hour walk with dog Blondi at 9:00 AM, followed by the main daily military situation conference that began at noon and lasted until about 2:00 PM.

Generally, the briefings covered distinct categories: the OKW theaters of war (North Africa, Norway, Finland, and Occupied France), and the OKH theater—which was the major one—the Eastern Front. There, OKW coordinated operations, but the general staff executed them.

According to Dr. Raiber,

> Contrary to legend, Hitler's "morning" briefing conferences had never convened in bunkers at the Wolfsschanze. From June 1941 until July 1942—when the FHQ transferred to Werwolf, just north of Vinnitsa in Ukraine—they met in a wooden annex built off the eastern side of Bunker #7 (Keitel Bunker). Upon their return to the Wolfsschanze in November 1942, and until February 1944, they were held in the wooden east wing of Bunker #11.

Here is Speer's own description of the very epicenter of the complex: "The conferences . . . took place in the situation room of the headquarters, adjacent to Hitler's private apartment. It was a modestly furnished room about 900 square feet in area, the walls paneled in light-colored wood."

During the reinforcement of Hitler's bunker in 1944, the daily briefings were moved again, this time to the so-called *lagebaracke* (briefing barracks). In this situation building, the famous July 20, 1944, attempt on Hitler's life occurred.

A two-hour-long luncheon followed the briefing if

time allowed, but after a furious quarrel with his major officers in September 1942, Hitler no longer dined with them as he had previously, choosing instead to eat either alone or with a few elite guests. Following lunch, Hitler napped, rested, and read. This brief respite was followed by a one-hour evening briefing at 6:00 PM (later at 9:00 PM) in the Führerbunker. Dinner was at 7:30 PM, followed by evening tea at 8:00 PM, which many times lasted into the early hours of the morning, ending as late as 2:00–3:00 AM.

On January 27, 1944, Hitler invited all his serving field marshals to Wolfsschanze for a major political address to prepare them for the expected Allied invasion of France as well as the Red Army summer offensive (that would destroy German Army Group Center). Knowing the turning point of the entire war would then be at hand, Hitler evoked images of Frederick the Great when he asserted, "If ever there comes a final hour, then I hope that you—my generals—will stand together on the barricades and that you—my field marshals—stand beside me with your swords drawn!"

Perhaps for reasons of health, Hitler preferred his office to be cold at FHQ Wolfsschanze. As recalled later by his last secretary, Traudl Junge, in *Until the Final Hour*, "They told me that Hitler only felt well at that temperature [52 degrees Fahrenheit] and never let it get any warmer in his workrooms. Now it was clear to me why the General Staff officers and the generals themselves always came out of the conferences—which often lasted for hours—with red noses and blue frozen hands." Perhaps it also reflected his earlier lifestyle and his years of poverty, both in Vienna and Munich. Or was this yet another actor's trick to gain a physical, if not a moral, ascendancy over his commanders?

The fear of air raids sometimes caused great confusion and dismay at Wolfsschanze, as revealed in the memoir of Traudl Junge: "The warnings were terrible at night. All the lights were suddenly switched off, everyone had to make haste to the bunkers. . . . We all had to know the password and the counter-password, for the guards weren't taking any nonsense, and would shoot faster than you could think." This was all born out of Hitler's concern over a surprise enemy parachute drop to seize the entire complex. "By now [1944], a huge apparatus had been constructed. There were barriers and new guard posts everywhere, miles of tangled barbed wire, watchtowers. The paths along which I had walked my dog one day would suddenly be blocked the next, with a guard wanting to see my pass."

Related Headquarters of State, Party, and Armed Forces Near FHQ Wolfsschanze, 1941–45

While FHQ Wolfsschanze was located near Rastenburg, OKH Headquarters Mauerwald (named for

the local forestry house) was near Lake Mauersee eleven miles north of Hitler's FHQ. It was home to both the Army High Command and the General Staff.

Camp Mauerwald was near Angerburg and was connected to Rastenburg both by a paved highway and a single trolley car line (*draisine* or *treibwagen*, according to Dr. Raiber). According to Peter Hoffmann in *Hitler's Personal Security*, in 1942, a colonel bound for Mauerwald got off the trolley at the Wolfsschanze by mistake, stumbled into Security Area 1, and was having breakfast in the officers' mess when the Führer's naval adjutant discovered him by chance. "He refused to believe that he was in Wolfsschanze until Puttkamer pointed out to him Hitler, exercising his dog [Blondi]."

Camp Mauerwald was divided into two parts—codenamed Fritz (General Staff) and Quelle (which means wellspring or source fountain)—and contained the General Staff's logistics section with its administrative offices in bunkers and huts.

Other nearby, related headquarters included OKL Robinson (Göring's Luftwaffe site) at Rominten in East Prussia, two hours distant from FHQ Wolfsschanze; Himmler's SS headquarters, Hochwald, near Grosgarten, and forty-five minutes by road from Hitler's own; and von Ribbentrop's Foreign Ministry field headquarters at Castle Steinort, ninety minutes by car from the FHQ. The OKM first under Raeder; then after 1943, Dönitz) remained in Berlin throughout the war. Dr. Lammers's Reich Chancellery HQ was at Rosengarten, five and a half miles northeast of Wolfsschanze. By highway, the OKH was an hour away from FHQ Wolfsschanze.

On October 5, 1941, Hitler made his sole visit to Mauerwald to see Field Marshal von Brauchitsch. The OKH stayed at Mauersee until the start of December 1944, when it relocated to Camp Maybach close to Zossen.

Army engineers disabled all of the various headquarters of the German State and Armed Forces with dynamite in January 1945 to prevent their future use by the Red Army. The Soviets later assumed control of Army HQ Zossen outside Berlin from 1945 to 1995.

Some Selected FHQ Costs

On September 22, 1944, Speer reported to Hitler's Armed Forces adjutant that 36 million Reichsmarks (RM) had thus far been spent on FHQ Wolfsschanze, another 13 million (RM) for the unused FHQ Siegfried/Hagen location, and a whopping 130 million (RM) more still for the also unused and largest FHQ, Riese.

According to Siedler and Ziegert in *Hitler's Secret Headquarters*, "The main FührerBunker cost 1.35 million RM, five times the amount required for the ante-Bunker (*Vorbunker*)," in Berlin underneath the grounds of the Old RC–New RC complex.

Based on these financial facts, it is a safe prediction

that had the war lasted until 1950—as Hitler expected—the costs of future FHQs across Europe (and maybe into Asia and the Middle East?) would have grown exponentially, as Hitler's power and fiscal resources likewise expanded.

Some Final Thoughts on Wolfsschanze

To visit the former FHQ today, Dr. Raiber recommended early November, when most of the leaves in the Görlitz Forest have fallen—and the other foliage is also minimal—so that all the buildings and bunkers are visible, despite the swampy, stagnant lowland setting.

Access to the interiors of the big bunkers beyond their entrance corridors is impossible. In most instances, this is because the heavy roofs collapsed when FHQ Wolfsschanze was demolished . . . in January 1945. In other cases, it appears the Poles later may have destroyed passages into some of the remaining interiors so that visitors would not be endangered by collapsing masonry. . . . Only the barest traces remain of the security fences.

The Führer Bunker ruin in Restricted Area 1 is most impressive. Originally, the Führer Bunker had been nothing more than a concrete house to which wooden and brick sections were appended. Additions were made to it during the second [1943] Wolfsschanze construction period, and again beginning in spring 1944. An enormous new central part emerged from this reconstruction.

In this last renovation, its walls and roof were reinforced by adding another shell of concrete, the two layers being separated by a space—often containing gravel fill—the purpose of which was to cushion the effect of hits by the heaviest bombs then known. The original ceilings are reported to have been about three meters thick, and four more meters were said to have been added in 1944.

We measured slabs of ceiling 4.8 meters thick, so it may well be that the total thickness exceeded seven meters plus the air/gravel space between the sheaths. We estimated the height of the central part of the Führer Bunker as about 14 meters. The massive central part is flanked by less heavily constructed east and west wings, the roofs of which have collapsed to within two or three meters of the ground.

In the east wing, furring strips which once supported interior paneling, as well as the remains of what was once was a Führer Bunker fireplace, can be seen. The original Führer Bunker windows were covered over when the 1944 outer shell of concrete was poured so that the north face now [1977] presents a sheer, naked concrete wall, canted slightly from the vertical and pierced only by two door way apertures which had been fitted with double steel doors, the latter subsequently salvaged by the local Poles just after the war.

Behind the north face of the Führer Bunker's central part, the giant structure had been gutted by the demolition charges which were set off in its bowels. Although the visitor is overwhelmingly impressed by the sheer enormity of the ruins, one is equally stunned when contemplating the magnitude of the explosive charges which must have been necessary to have ripped them apart so violently.

Huge fragments of steel laced concrete—often as large as small houses—were avulsed, and now lie appreciable distances from their origins. A large crack has rent the immense north face of the Führer Bunker from top to bottom, and its side walls have been convulsed, twisted, and thrust into unbelievable bias for such huge masses of reinforced concrete.

The thick roof behind the north face—above the site where the main charge must have been sown—has simply disappeared! (It took two full days—January 23–25, 1945—to complete Operation Inselsprung.)

The Führer Bunker's central part measured 37 meters across, and the east and west wings added another 25 meters. The height was estimated at over 13.5 meters . . .

Wooden cleats—to which camouflage nets were attached 5–6 meters high—are still [1977] visible on some trees. . . . Most of the concrete covered brick barracks type buildings, the most common Wolfsschanze structures, were mined so that their roofs simply collapsed, rendering them unusable.

Dr. Raiber concluded, "There is one swamp no less than 100 meters from the Führer Bunker . . . with hordes of flies, mosquitoes, and other creatures for whom the marshlands were the natural habitat." Even Hitler called the Görlitz Forest the worst possible location to have placed his most important field command post of the entire war!

(Far Left) This is an aerial test photograph taken in 1942 to verify the effectiveness of camouflage at Wolfsschanze. *HHA*

(Above) The Führer's hand on the back of his Ju-52 aircraft seat over Poland, September 11, 1939.

TO OUTER SECURITY
BARRIER SPERRKREIS II

SAUNA
26

TYPISTS' OFFICES
25

SS ESCORT DETACHMENT/
HITLER'S PERSONAL SERVANTS
23

DETECTIVE DETAIL/
POST OFFICE
24

PARKING

SECURITY FENCE
FÜHRERSPERRKREIS (July 1944)

DETECTIVE SECURITY DETAIL
22

GUESTS' BUNKER
(reinforced 1944)
15

GOVERNMENT AND SERVICE
LIAISON OFFICERS, DOCTORS
BARBERS, ETC.

SS ESCORT DETACHMENT
BARRACKS (built 1944)
61

RSD and SS
BARRACKS
21

SITUATION CONFERENCES

VON STAUFFENBERG'S
BOMB EXPLODED HERE
20

FÜHRER SPERRKREIS GATE

TELEPRINTER
EXCHANGE
(reinforced 1944)
16

40
BUNKER

39

BUNKER
63

62

1

REICH PRESS BUNKER

GARAGES

BUNKER

MODERN PARKING AREA

SECURITY FENCE
SPERRKREIS I

WESTERN
ENTRANCE

TO BAHNHOF GÖRLITZ
AND RASTENBURG

VON STAUFFENBERG'S
EXIT ROUTE

TO RASTENBURG

OFFICERS GUARD POST
58

LIAISON OFFICE VON RIBBENTROP
55

BARRACKS
59

56

VON STAUFFENBERG'S
EXIT ROUTE

BUNKER
60

TO RASTENBURG AIRFIELD

(Left) East Prussian wartime road signpost near
Wolfsschanze. *HHA*

(Below) An overview of the inner security ring of
FHQ Wolfsschanze. *Reprinted with permission from
After the Battle*

(Above) A previously unpublished view of the Wolfsschanze commuter trolley, which Dr. Raiber also called "the self-propelled rail shuttle car [*draisine*, or *treibwagen*]." *Treibwagen* is translated as rail motor, prime mover, or motor coach. According to von Stahlberg in *Bounden Duty*, "The evening briefing with Hitler generally began between 9–10 PM. In deep darkness, we got into a train consisting of only one or two carriages, which was waiting by the guest house [at Mauerwald/Angerburg] to take us in 10–15 minutes directly into the innermost restricted area of the Wolf's Lair." Schmundt is at right. *HHA*

(Above) Field Marshal Walther von Brauchitsch, commander in chief of the German Army, climbs aboard the trolley during the summer of 1941, as two railway men look on in this previously unpublished view. *HHA*

(Above) A good side view of the car with its leader. *LC*

(Left) A good side view of the trolley car. *LC*

(Left) A rare and previously unpublished view of Hitler and the Duce on the inside of the trolley car on their way either to or from German Army Headquarters. Note the odd-looking buildings outside the window. *HHA*

(Right) The trolley arrives at Army HQ Mauerwald at Angerburg, East Prussia, during Mussolini's visit of August 25–29, 1941. The Duce (right) shakes hands with Col. Gen Franz Halder (left), as von Brauschitsch (back to camera) salutes Hitler with his marshal's interim baton; a saluting Hitler is followed by Italian Army Marshal Ugo Cavallero, who in turn is followed by Schmundt. At left a Reichsbahn official gives a Nazi salute. *HHA*

(Right) A previously unpublished photo of the Rastenburg swimming hole, where Hans Baur went fishing from his VW Kubelwagen (bucket car) and where Rommel and his staff officers stole von Manstein's and von Stahlberg's clothes while they were in the water, as a boyish prank. *HHA*

(Below right) A very rare shot, indeed, of Hitler's *first* dog at FHQ Wolfsschanze. From left to right are: von Ribbentrop, Hitler, and his Scottish terrier, Burli. Hitler gave the dog to Eva Braun's mother, Franziska, in Munich sometime either late in 1942 or early in 1943. *JRA*

(Below) Hitler's daily exercise consisted of a walk in a small strip of land next to the Führerbunker of less than one hundred yards with his Alsatian or German shepherd dog, Blondi, and then putting her through her paces (as seen here in August 1943). *HHA*

(*Left*) An RSD guard on duty within Restricted Area 1 at Wolfsschanze, wearing a protective anti-mosquito head netting with a typical one-story bunker as a backdrop (left). Traudl Junge described summer weather at FHQ Wolfsschanze in *Until the Final Hour*, "We could hardly breathe in the camp huts, and we preferred to work in the bunkers, where it was much cooler. Mosquitoes and flies made life outside almost unbearable. . . . Hitler loathed the weather. He no longer went out with Blondi, whom he entrusted to Sgt.-Maj. Fritz Tornow, the official in charge of looking after the dogs. He was perpetually in a bad mood, and complained of migraines and insomnia; his need for relaxation became ever more pressing. . . ." In addition to that, the Army—in an attempt to kill all the mosquitoes—poured oil on the lakes, thus destroying all the frogs along with the insects. Hitler was upset because he enjoyed hearing the frogs croaking as he fell asleep, so more frogs had to be brought in for this purpose. *HHA*

(*Left*) A pair of RSD guards resting on a wooden park bench next to a bunker. *HHA*

(*Below*) The RSD watch (left) gives Hitler the Nazi salute as his Mercedes-Benz G-4 passes through Restricted Area 1 Officers Guard Post (or Guard Post 1). According to Dr. Raiber, the vehicle "is just turning north to enter Restricted Area 1 through its western gate [out of the photograph on the right]." Hitler sits up front, next to his regular chauffeur, Kempka. *HHA*

(Above) An entrance gate checkpoint, in a previously unpublished photo, as it looked in 1998, fifty-three years after the end of the war. *John H. Bloecher, Jr., DSG*

(Above) An excellent view of rooftop camouflage atop bunkers at FHQ Wolfsschanze, 1942. Dr. Raiber described these fake "trees" as "a long pole from which multiple wooden arms projected at various levels and in different directions, and over which a camouflage net had been suspended." *HHA*

(Above) A previously unpublished side view of a typical, camouflaged one-story bunker (#6, a guest bunker) with steel door and window shutters opened, as an officer enters. Note, too, the "tree" planted on the roof at upper left to confuse enemy aircraft. It was greatly reinforced with extra concrete in 1944. *HHA*

(Above) Hitler goes over a document with Schmundt (right) outside Bunker #7, the Keitel Bunker, perhaps just before or after the daily noontime briefing inside. In the winter of 1942, the briefings were held in the Keitel Bunker. This previously unpublished shot provides an excellent view of a typical bunker doorway, complete with steel doors and identifying numbers. *HHA*

(Above) Mussolini (left) in Italian Army First Marshal of the Empire uniform and cap during his August 25, 1941, visit with Hitler at Wolfsschanze. *HHA*

(Right) Outside Bunker #10, Kasino 1, from left to right: press chief Dr. Dietrich, Keitel, and Hitler in the summer of 1941. *HHA*

(Left) A pair of RSD guards outside Hitler's Führerbunker, #11, on patrol during Count Ciano's visit of October 25, 1941. *HHA*

(Right) A view from inside the Führerbunker at FHQ *Wolfsschanze* while looking through the open door of the screened-in front porch, with a vigilant RSD officer on-post outside, summer 1941. *HHA*

(Right) The exact opposite of the previously unpublished view, looking toward the front of the Führerbunker from outside. Approaching the cameraman, from left to right: Luftwaffe General of the Fighters Adolf Galland, Keitel, Hitler, and Field Marshal Erhard Milch in the winter of 1941–42. *HHA*

(Right) Göring (left) and von Brauchitsch at Wolfsschanze on September 18, 1941. In 1938 Hitler named the latter commander in chief of the Army over the former, but when he forced von Brauchitsch's resignation on December 19, 1941, Hitler took over the post for the rest of the war. Note Göring's interim Reich Marshal's baton, still missing today. *HGA*

(Left) In a pair of previously unpublished photographs, Hitler is greeted by his Rastenburg staff under the pine trees; note the camouflage netting overhead. In the top photo, Keitel stands second from left, while in the bottom photo are, from left to right: Linge, Hitler, Keitel, and Dönitz, who was not yet promoted to grand admiral, giving a Nazi salute without his future baton of office. *HHA*

(Left) From left to right: an unknown SS man, Linge, Artur Kannenberg, Hitler, and newsreel cameraman Walter Frentz at work. The date is possibly July 20, 1944, as Hitler is wearing the black rain cape seen in many other photos of that day after the failed Army Bomb Plot. *HHA*

(Left) The Führerbunker and new annex following the second construction period of late fall 1942, as seen from the left side rear. *HHA*

(Below) The same structure, following reinforcement work, in the fall of 1944, shortly before Hitler left the FHQ for good on November 20. *HHA*

(Right) Hitler's expanded Führerbunker under construction, where—from February 23 to July 16, 1944—its ceiling was reinforced to a thickness of 8 meters. *HHA*

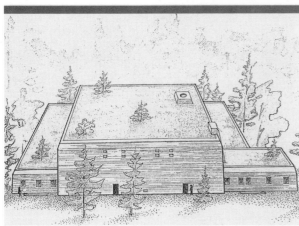

(Left) An excellent artist's rendering of the Führerbunker, where the July 20, 1944, conference was supposed to be held but wasn't because it was still under construction. Note the camouflage, as well as the scale of the size of the building (four stories), as shown by the small figure at center right. *Waroslaw Zarzecki*

(Above) The Gastebunker (guest bunker), where Hitler lived during mid-July–November 1944. Note the entrance steps at lower right and the camouflage "trees" at left and right. *HHA*

(Above) From left to right are: Keitel, Hitler, and Linge walking directly in front of the guest bunker toward the map hut, #3. *HHA*

(Top) The Führerbunker, as it appeared in 1998. The bunker is too large to fit in one photograph, so this is a composite of two separate previously unpublished pictures. The wide crack at the left was caused by the January 1945 German Army engineers' demolition attempt. The painted #13 at the left is to be totally ignored, according to the late Dr. Raiber in 1977 in *After the Battle*: "The numbers, etc., above the doorway are phony, painted for a recent [1974] Polish motion picture filmed 'on location.' No original inscriptions on the bunkers survive." *John H. Bloecher, Jr., DSG*

(Above) A seated RSD man checks the identification card of Col. Schmundt (left) against the registry book on the table inside one of the bunkers. Note the open steel door with handles at left. Overall security was tightened after the failed Army Bomb Plot explosion of July 20, 1944, and all briefcases were examined for the first time during the war and all side arms were confiscated. It was a great shock that a serving military officer would try to kill Hitler, an unheard of occurrence in modern German history. *HHA*

(Right) A modern, self-dialing telephone exchange at FHQ Wolfsschanze is seen in this previously unpublished photo. Writing in *Hitler Was My Friend,* Hoffmann recalled an incident in which he told Hitler of Churchill's arrival at Cairo. When the Führer demanded to know how his photographer knew that, the latter lied, stating, "Oh, a couple of SS men whom I met on the way here told me." The angry Hitler immediately summoned Himmler from HQ Hochwald thirty miles away, and a lineup of SS men from the telephone exchange was formed after Hitler

concluded that was the source of the leak. None admitted to it, however, and it was soon deduced that Hoffmann had broken security by listening to the forbidden BBC radio broadcast from London. *HHA*

(Below right) Officers watched over the telephone operators around the clock, as seen here. Listening in on conversations was forbidden, but it happened anyway. In one celebrated incident, the RFSS himself was chastised severely for discussing the Holocaust with Martin Bormann over an open line. *HHA*

(Left) A previously unpublished photograph of the Wolfsschanze telex station, with SS men transcribing foreign broadcasts for review by the operations staff. Note the Siemens T38 series teletype machine on the table in the corner. If people making outgoing telephone calls had poor connections, they sent telex messages instead. A telex is a message sent electronically to a teleprinter, which prints it out in typed format. The system prepares, stores, and transmits messages, but it has now been replaced by modern email. *HHA*

(Left) A good photo of the Wolfsschanze barbershop. Kaiserhof Hotel barber, August Wollenhaupt (left), came to Wolfsschanze to cut Hitler's hair, as well as that of his entourage. *HHA*

(Right) From left to right, in May 1941: von Ribbentrop, Hitler, former Iraqi Prime Minister Rashid Ali al Gailani (after he was forced from office by the British Army because of his pro-Axis regime), and an aide. Gailani spent the rest of the war as a refugee in Nazi Germany. *HHA*

(Right) Mussolini (left, in civilian suit) poses with Göring (right) at Wolfsschanze after his rescue from captivity by SS Maj. Otto Skorzeny on September 12, 1943. When Hitler asked Skorzeny if enemy paratroopers could take Wolfsschanze, Skorzeny said yes and confirmed Hitler's fears. *HHA*

(Left) Fellow Austrians—Skorzeny and Hitler—pose for a victory shot at Wolfsschanze following the successful rescue of Mussolini from atop the Gran Sasso mountain in Italy on September 12, 1943. *HHA*

(Below) Hitler's Armed Forces adjutant from 1938–44, Schmundt, gives the Rastenburg staff a map briefing. Seated with backs to camera are, from left to right: two unknown men, Dr. Brandt, Martin Bormann, unknown man, Keitel, and Schaub. According to Warlimont in *Inside Hitler's Headquarters*, Hitler's personal maps were locked up in his own office desk. *HHA*

(Left) A typical wartime map briefing as seen in a previously unpublished photo taken in the Keitel Bunker at Wolfsschanze. From left to right: von Ribbentrop, unknown officer, Jodl, Keitel, Hitler, Hungarian Prime Minister Miklós Kallay, and Warlimont. Hitler's standing dictum was, "I alone carry the responsibility, and no one else!" But Warlimont's 1964 lament, noted in *Inside Hitler's Headquarters*, was that the generals couldn't get him to make a decision, and when he did, "his decisions were all too often overtaken by events." *HHA*

(Middle) The FHQ's sauna room (building #26, completed May 24, 1942), which Hitler had installed for his associates as a precaution against colds and chills but which he never used himself. *HHA*

(Below) A Berliner named Otto Günther and nicknamed "Krumel" (Crumbs) was an FHQ cook on loan from the Hotel Mitropa. Günther was only allowed to serve the residents of Wolfsschanze the same field rations eaten by German troops. Over the kitchen door Günther placed a sign reading, "Who does not honor Crumbs is not worthy of the cake!" according to Traudl Junge in *Until the Final Hour*. He angered vegetarian Hitler, however, by sometimes serving him secret bits of meat, fat, and broth. Hitler always rebuked him and demanded instead only gruel, mashed potatoes, and other nonmeat dishes. This is a photo of Hitler's very own kitchen at Wolfsschanze, showing, from left to right: an unknown woman, cook Günther, and Traudl Junge (seated). There was an official list of thirty-eight people who were authorized to eat with Hitler. *HHA*

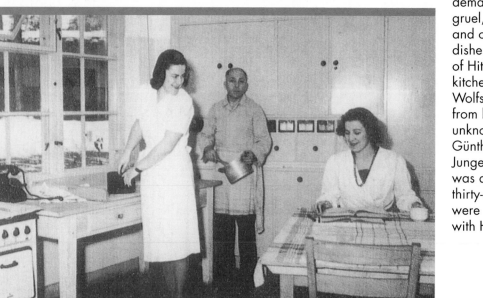

(Left) A mess hall at
Wolfsschanze.
Stated von Stahlberg
in *Bounden Duty*, "To
watch Hitler eating
was . . . edifying to
me. His left arm
rested on his thigh
while his right, the
elbow propped on
the table, moved the
spoon to and fro along the shortest
possible route between bowl and
mouth. . . . I asked von Manstein
what Hitler could have been eating
from his special dish. 'A thin veg-
etable soup,' he said, and that was
all he would say." *HHA*

(Middle) One of the FHQ's many
meeting rooms. *HHA*

(Bottom) A typical FHQ office/living
area with a radio at the far end of the
room. *HHA*

(Right) A previously unpublished photograph of a standard double bedroom with shared table and closed blackout curtains. *HHA*

(Left) Dr. Otto Dietrich (left) and German News Bureau (DNB) Chief Heinz Lorenz (right), his deputy, preparing a news release on Wehrmacht operations for wartime media outlets. *HHA*

(Left) A good wide-angle view of Hitler's personal office at FHQ Wolfsschanze. Hitler moved back into the rebuilt Führerbunker on November 8, 1944, but left it for good a mere twelve days later. *HHA*

(Left) A curtained-off, smaller private meeting room of Hitler's in front of an open fireplace at Wolfsschanze. *HHA*

(Middle) A "photo op" wartime meeting in Hitler's office with von Below (back to camera), Luftwaffe ace Hans-Joachim Marseille (the famed "Star of Africa," later killed), and Hitler in this previously unpublished photograph. *HHA*

(Bottom) On July 1, 1942, Hitler presented Erich von Manstein (center) with the coveted baton of a field marshal in the German Army (in the black box on the map table between them), as von Puttkamer looks on at right in this previously unpublished picture. Today, many historians consider von Manstein the best German strategist of the war. His fellow marshals wanted him appointed commander in chief of the Eastern Front, but Hitler always refused. Fired by Hitler in 1944, von Manstein saw no further military service for the rest of the war. *HHA*

(Left) In the very same room but on another occasion, Hitler presents his 1942–44 commander in chief West, von Rundstedt (left), with another medal in this previously unpublished photo. *HHA*

(Right) In the same room on yet another occasion, with, from left to right: an unknown soldier, Sepp Dietrich, SS General Fegelein (obscured, behind column), Gunsche, unknown Army officer, and Hitler. Note Hitler's oversized magnifying glass (lower right) on the map table. *HHA*

(Bottom right) An openair meeting area at FHQ Wolfsschanze, most likely either Building #30—the Old Teahouse—or #10, the New Teahouse. All of Hitler's field headquarters featured such teahouses. *HHA*

10 FHQ WERWOLF, VINNITSA, UKRAINE, 1942–1943

On July 16, 1942, the Führer moved his headquarters further east—to Vinnitsa in German-occupied Ukraine—to be nearer to the two summer offensives toward Stalingrad and into the oil-rich Caucasus. Originally known as Anlage Eichenhain (Installation, or Camp, Oak Grove), upon his arrival that day, Hitler immediately changed its name to FHQ Werwolf (Armed Wolf). In June, this FHQ and FHQ Barenhöhle (Cave or Den)—also on Soviet territory—was almost finished. A third FHQ, Wasserburg (Water Mountain), was located in Estonia. Hitler, however, never spent a single day at either Barenhöhle or Wasserburg.

In all, Hitler passed one hundred days at FHQ Werwolf, making it his third-longest stay at any single field headquarters after FHQ Wolfsschanze and FHQ Berghof. FHQ Werwolf resembled a quaint, rustic summer camp rather than a major command center in a world war. Yet it was there that Hitler made one of the war's most fateful decisions and against OKH advice: he split Army Group South in half with two separate but simultaneous objectives. These goals were to take both Stalingrad and the Caucasus, rather than one or the other—as his generals urged him to do—thus greatly diminishing his overall military strength in both campaigns.

As a result, it was also at FHQ Werwolf that the Führer began what amounted to a two-and-a-half-year period of arguments back and forth with his field marshals and generals over the strategic and even the tactical direction of the war.

Description of FHQ Werwolf

The installation consisted of nineteen fortified blockhouses that appeared finished on the outside, but the cement hadn't yet dried completely on the inside. In addition were RSD and Luftwaffe barracks, huts, and cabins for the camp's staff and security forces.

Writing in *Inside the Third Reich* in 1970, Speer described the setting:

> Instead of the usual concrete buildings, a pleasant looking cluster of blockhouses scattered about a forest was established. . . .

> In contrast to the luxuriously furnished dining hall in the Chancellery, this dining room looked rather like the railroad station restaurant in a small town.

Added Jan Zduniak and Klaus-Jurgen Ziegler in *Wolf's Lair and Hitler's Other Headquarters*, "There were air raid bunkers and brick buildings, as well as wooden houses and barracks; it was surrounded by a high fence and barbed wire." Baur disputed this in *Hitler at My Side*:

> Our relations with the local civil population were excellent. . . .The place was not even surrounded by barbed wire, and remained open on all sides until—much later on—partisans turned up in the neighborhood of Berlitchev, about 45 miles away.

Upon Hitler's arrival, the FHQ commandant—Col. Kurt Thomas—gave him a tour of the facility, and they went into the antechamber of the Führer House, where a map of European Russia was painted on wood and hung on the wall. Then they inspected the camp's security: a defensive ring of bunkers, minefields, tanks, antiaircraft guns, and even antitank ditches in case the Red Army broke through and attacked.

In his spare time at FHQ Werwolf, Hitler read the works of Robert Graves: *I, Claudius* and *Claudius the God*. The heat and his generals irritated him immensely. According to *The Hitler Book*, "A fly on the wall could send him into a rage, and he would be beside himself with fury at the appearance of a harmless butterfly. Everything was done to prevent flies, midges or butterflies from coming near him."

Related Headquarters

As with FHQ Wolfsschanze, both Göring and Himmler had field headquarters close to FHQ Werwolf, with Göring's command bunker being about twelve miles away from Vinnitsa. Himmler established Hegewald (Forest Preserve or Nursery), also called Hochwald (Timber Forest or High Woods), at Zhitomir, about thirty miles north of FHQ Werwolf. Previously, Hegewald had been code-named Solu and Waldhof (Forest Court). Foreign Minister von Ribbentrop also had a Ukrainian headquarters. Of the trio of complexes, that of the RFSS was the most interesting, for it established a direct link for the first time between not only Hegewald and FHQ Werwolf but also with the Holocaust against the Jews and others.

The Holocaust and FHQ Werwolf

According to Richard Rhodes in his work *Masters of Death: The SS Einsatzgruppen and the Invention of the Holocaust,* by September 4, 1941, the entire area radiating out from the forward FHQ had been made "Jew free" for a full forty miles in all directions. "In April 1942, the remaining Jews of Vinnitsa were assembled at the local stadium for a selection. Hitler would not occupy Werwolf until mid-July, but it was time to tidy up. . . . The Germans killed the children separately at Vinnitsa." Von Manstein's aide—Alexander von Stahlberg (part Jewish himself)—also mentioned this in his work, *Bounden Duty.*

As this book was being written, a new study appeared that confirmed what authors Rhodes and Stahlberg maintained earlier. In her 2005 study *Nazi Empire-Building and the Holocaust in Ukraine,* Wendy Lower asserted that both FHQ Werwolf and the RFSS Hegewald/Hochwald were built by forced Jewish slave labor. Furthermore, she also tied Dr. Fritz Todt of the Organization Todt to Himmler and the Holocaust directly, because at Hitler's headquarters the OT used Jewish slave laborers, who were murdered after its completion.

> **The timing of the building and the eventual arrival of Hitler and other elites to the region coincided with the major killing actions around Zhitomir and Vinnitsa. . . . Local SS and police were pressured to "clear" the area before the arrival of Hitler, Himmler, and the other Nazi chiefs. . . . The use of Jews as laborers fulfilled a short term German need and also provided SD personnel with an "acceptable" pretext for killing the Jewish laborers who had worked at the sites. They argued that all of the Jewish laborers and their families must die as an extra "security precaution."**

According to *The Hitler Book*, the Führer agreed: "'Who built the camp?' [A colonel] answered, 'Mostly Russian prisoners from the camps.' Hitler's face darkened. He told Thomas, 'They must all be shot! There is not a moment to lose. They know too much about my HQ.'" The Russians' sources for this story were their POWs Linge, Gunsche, and Baur.

Added Seidler and Ziegert in *Hitler's Secret Headquarters*, "During the Second World War, 12.9 million working days—each lasting between eight and 16 hours—would be expended on building FHQs. As the war progressed, the OT work force expanded to 1.5 million. . . . Added to this figure were the prisoners-of-war." In effect, slave labor—altogether a veritable army in itself—built ever more command centers. This huge waste of labor, materials, and finances could well have been better used elsewhere.

Planned Conquest and SS Settlement of Russia to the Ural Mountains

RFSS Himmler arrived at Forest Preserve on July 24, 1942, and duly met with Hitler at FHQ Werwolf the very next day, according to Dr. Lower. Noted Rhodes in *Masters of Death*, "In a meeting at *Werwolf* in mid-July 1942 . . . Hitler had endorsed the Reichsführer's [Himmler's] plan for clearing out the east and colonizing it." General Plan East represented nothing less than the complete repopulation of the entire conquered former USSR to the Ural Mountains, with 4.5 million German settlers moving in over the three decades of 1943 to 1973, according to Rhodes.

Himmler called it "the greatest piece of colonization which the world will have ever seen," in his excited words to his Finnish masseur, Dr. Felix Kersten (*Memoirs*). Indeed, Dr. Lower stated that, in effect, Himmler's own headquarters at Hegewald/Hochwald was his first such experiment, an SS island of racial purity in a sea of Soviet Ukrainian Jewry.

Hitler, too, was having his own delusions of grandeur at about this same time, as recalled by Speer in 1976 in *Spandau: The Secret Diaries*:

> **In the middle of August 1942 . . . after one of the conferences, Hitler sat on a bench at a plain deal table, in the shade of the trees surrounding his frame bungalow. . . . In his low voice . . . Hitler began: "For a long time, I have had everything prepared. As the next step, we are going to advance south of the Caucasus and then help the rebels in Iran and Iraq against the English. . . . Another thrust will be directed against the Caspian Sea toward Afghanistan and India, then the English will run out of oil. In two years [i.e., by 1944] we'll be on the borders of India; 20–30 elite German divisions will do. Then the British Empire will collapse."**

This was the high tide of Nazi conquest, but already Hitler's reach had far exceeded his grasp. The grandiose dream of the RFSS's General Plan East was never to be. The surrender of the German Sixth Army at Stalingrad the following February 2, 1943, put it on ice forever.

Meanwhile, Hitler met not only with his RFSS and the Reich Marshal at FHQ Werwolf but with his Axis Pact partners as well, to keep them in line.

Visiting Axis Pact Heads of State and Foreign Ministers

Both foreign heads of state Dr. Ante Pavelic of the independent State of Croatia and Marshal Ion Antonescu of Romania visited FHQ Werwolf during the months of July through September 1942.

Toward the end of 1942, both foreign ministers Count Ciano of Fascist Italy and Pierre Laval of Vichy France visited Hitler at FHQ Werwolf as the year ended on a sour political-military note. The former had suggested to Hitler for the first time on the Duce's behalf that—in concert with the looming disasters at Stalingrad and in North Africa—it might be wise to seek peace with Stalin at least, if not also the West.

Hitler declined, and the war went on. These overall failures in the military situation, in the end, determined everything.

Hitler's Clashes with Halder and Jodl

Warlimont credited Col. Gen. Franz Halder, chief of the German General Staff—not the Führer—with being the real genius behind the first successful campaign in Russia. In the summer of 1942, however, Hitler began moving individual divisions himself, from his map table telephone.

In *Adolf Hitler*, Toland recorded Warlimont's observations of Hitler's Army commanders:

> **He recalled how petrified Keitel had become the time Hitler angrily threw a file on the table. As it tumbled to the floor, (Keitel) stood petrified as if he were a junior officer. It was a typical case, Warlimont thought, "of a man given a position for which he was unqualified."**

In his own memoir, Keitel asserted he never wanted the (OKW) top job and would have preferred instead the active field command that Hitler never gave him.

Colonel General Halder, however, was quite different. It was at FHQ Werwolf that he and Hitler had their clash of August 24, 1942, that a month later led to the former's removal from office. Among others, Seidler and Ziegert in *Hitler's Secret Headquarters* noted the following exchange:

> Hitler: **I expect from the commanders the same hardness as from the troops at the front!**

> Halder: **I take your point, mein Führer, but out there, brave musketeers and lieutenants are falling in their thousands simply because the High Command [i.e., Hitler personally] cannot order the only possible solution, and their hands are tied.**
> Hitler: **Col. Gen. Halder, what sort of tone is that to use to me? You are telling me what it is like for the man at the front? What is your experience of being at the front? Where were you in the First World War? And you reproach me by saying I don't know what it is like at the front! I absolutely forbid it! I never heard of such a thing!**

Of this event, Warlimont noted in *Inside Hitler's Headquarters*, "The final breach between these two men who were as different as chalk from cheese could not be far off."

On September 7, 1942, Hitler sent Jodl on a fact-finding mission to see Field Marshal Wilhelm List in the Caucasus about the slow advance of his troops. When Jodl returned only to say that List was following Hitler's instructions, the Führer leaped to his feet and shouted, "That's a lie!" Then he angrily stalked out of the room, according to Warlimont.

On September 9, 1942, Hitler fired List, taking over personal command of Army Group A. Rumors flew that Keitel, Jodl, and Halder were also to be let go. While the first two were retained, Hitler replaced Halder as chief of the German General Staff with Gen. Kurt Zeitzler who, as had his predecessor, also stood up to an angry Führer. Unlike Halder, Zeitzler managed to restore the Army's influence, which had been missing at FHQ since Gen. Ludwig Beck was fired in 1938, and Zeitzler even managed to exclude Jodl and OKW from Eastern Front affairs.

Still, at all times, Hitler ensured that he alone was fully informed regarding all the varied theaters of war, thus successfully dividing and ruling all his underlings and staying in power until the very moment he shot himself in the right temple. Indeed, no man knew better than Hitler himself that Nazi Germany had lost the war.

While at FHQ Werwolf Hitler avoided his staff, going out of his sunless blockhouse only after dark and using the rear entrance to avoid being seen. The daily conferences were moved from the usual site to his Führer House, and only the most indispensable speakers were admitted in an icy atmosphere of as few words as possible. On September 12, 1942, Hitler had Bormann introduce a pair of Reichstag stenographers into each daily military situation conference from then until the end of the war. They copied down every single word that was spoken, and these transcripts were the charge of Bormann, Gen. Walter Scherff—the official Hitlerian war historian—and the various Führer adjutants. They were all under lock and key as well, as Hitler feared that the minutes might be either stolen or changed to damage his place in history. Even so, General Scherff himself destroyed many of the records as the war ended. Virtually all Hitler's surviving field marshals and generals blamed him in their postwar memoirs for the mistakes that they had jointly made. The exceptions were Keitel and Jodl, who both stood loyal to the end of their lives on October 16, 1946, at Nuremberg's gallows.

Hitler left FHQ Werwolf for the last time on March 13, 1943. The Kursk offensive against the Red Army failed that July, and in October von Manstein's Army Group South took over the former FHQ site as its own headquarters. Noted von Stahlberg in *Bounden Duty,*

> Our Operations Section took over the block-houses built for Hitler in a patch of woodland north of the town. From the outside, they were simple and rustic, but every comfort was provided inside. . . .The architect who had built this house had designed it with great skill. . . .The many photographs of Hitler in front of his house had never had to be touched up in

order to show him off to the public before his "modest little cottage." In fact, the house had an inner courtyard. . . . Hitler's suite at the back of the house contained a beautiful living room and study, bedroom, and bathrooms. . . . All the walls were paneled in pine, and there were a great many pictures of Hitler's suite.

And what was FHQ Werwolf's fate? Here is an extract from *Hitler and His Generals* regarding Hitler's military conference of December 27–28, 1943, as the Red Army approached the FHQ:

> He (von Manstein) must get out of Vinnitsa!... There must be a special detachment at Vinnitsa to burn the whole headquarters down and blow it up. It is most important (that) there should be no furniture left, otherwise the Russians will send it to Moscow and put it on display. Burn the lot!

It was done. But on December 31, 1943, the Forest Preserve headquarters of RFSS Himmler fell to the Red Army when Zhitomir was taken, followed by Vinnitsa and the ruins of FHQ Werwolf on March 20, 1944.

For some unknown reason, in mid-July 1942, Hitler (center) wears an overcoat in the Ukrainian summer heat as he inspects his FHQ location in occupied Soviet territory with Schmundt (far left) and FHQ Camp Commandant Col. Kurt Thomas (right). Note the log hut in the background at the far left. A portion of the OKH command staff left HQ *Mauerwald* and came to FHQ *Werwolf* with Hitler. Hitler left Vinnitsa on November 1, 1942, to speak at Munich. Then came the Allies' Operation Torch landings in North Africa, so the Führer returned to Wolfsschanze. He then went back to FHQ *Werwolf* early in 1943 to look over von Manstein's post-Stalingrad winter counteroffensive to halt the resurgent Red Army. Hitler left for good as site commander on March 13. *HHA*

(Top and above) The typical log cabin or hut construction style found at FHQ *Werwolf*. Note also the camouflaged netting overhead in both scenes. *HHA.*

(Right) Noted *After the Battle* in 1977, "One unusual feature was an extensive underground sentry post network throughout the wood," but this is an air-raid shelter entrance for Hitler and his suite. *HHA*

(Bottom) A Nazi outdoor conclave beside one of the wooden buildings at *Werwolf* on August 31, 1942; from left to right, von Ribbentrop, Göring, Milch (back to camera), and Göring's FHQ liaison officer, Luftwaffe Gen. Karl Bodenschatz. *Walter Frentz/ Signal Magazine*

(Left) From left to right are seen Col. Gen. Heinz Guderian, Hewel, Keitel, Bodenschatz, Hitler, Schaub, Milch, Speer, Dr. Morell, unknown SS officer, unidentified Foreign Office aide (with leather briefcase and envelope under his arm), Speer aide Willy Liebel, and two other unknown men at FHQ *Werwolf*. Speer was then running the German arms program following the death of Dr. Todt in February 1942. *Walter Frentz/Signal Magazine*

(Above) A previously unpublished photo of Luftwaffe Col. Gen. (later Field Marshal) Wolfram von Richthofen (left) and von Below (right) as they take a stroll at FHQ *Werwolf*. *HHA*

(Right) The Führer (center) and his entourage inspect the FHQ *Werwolf* swimming pool, which was never used, especially not by nonswimmer Hitler! It has also been cited as a "fire-fighter's pond" similar to the later 1945 "water tank" in the FHQ New RC park in Berlin. *HHA*

(Right) Hitler (center right) receives Dr. Ante Pavelic (center) as three unknown officers look on, with Hitler's own Führer House as the "photo op" backdrop on September 24, 1942—the very day that Halder was fired as chief of the German General Staff. The Nazi SS considered Dr. Pavelic's Croatian Ustashe (Rebel) thugs worse than themselves in terms of brutality in occupied Serbia during 1941–44. He escaped to South America after the war, with the Vatican's aid, and died peacefully in bed in Franco's Spain in 1957. *HHA*

(Above) The Führer's former personal living quarters, or Führer House, at Vinnitsa. It was later used (after Hitler's final departure) by von Manstein as his own residence and is seen here in July 1943 during the climactic Battle of Kursk, the largest tank battle to date in military history. Inside was where the daily situation meetings were convened after Hitler's argument with Jodl on September 7, 1942. *CER*

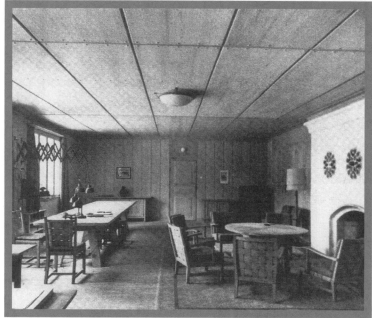

(Above) A good view of the more refined side of the Führer House at Vinnitsa that was not shown to the German public. Ironically, Hitler had come to FHQ *Werwolf* to personally direct the attack of the German Sixth Army at Stalingrad but then left eighteen days before the great Red Army counteroffensive that encircled the embattled city and also cut off the "attacking" Germans. The great crisis of the first half of the Second World War was at hand, but Hitler saw it instead as Stalin's doom, not his own. *Walter Frentz*

(Left) A superior, wide-angle view of the Führer's office at FHQ *Werwolf*, taken during his final stay there, February 19–March 13, 1943. It is seen from behind his own desk with a map table at left and a smaller conference table and seating area in front of the fireplace at right. FHQ *Werwolf* was almost one thousand kilometers closer to the Eastern Front than was Wolfsschanze at Rastenburg. *HHA*

(Above) Von Below's birthday party in September 1942, the same month that Hitler fired his second General Staff Chief, Col. Gen. Franz Halder. From left to right are: Hitler secretary Johanna Wolf (back to camera), von Below, Führer secretary Christa Schröder, SS Dr. Karl Brandt in Army uniform, Hewel in a pensive mood, Albert Bormann, and a laughing Julius Schaub, with an unknown Army officer at far right looking on. Note also the two extension lamps with accordion-like arms suspended overhead and behind the group. The blackout curtains are also shut. *HHA*

(Right) The Führer (right) shakes hands with Waffen SS Gen. Felix Steiner, who was later unable to rescue his besieged leader and Berlin in 1945. *HHA*

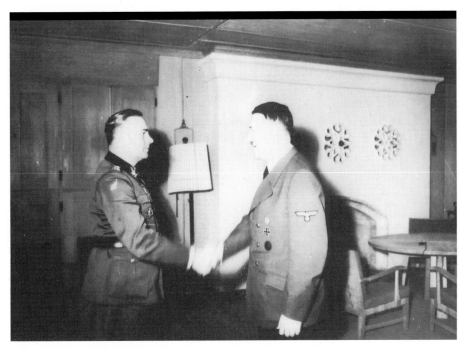

A birthday party for Martin Bormann's secretary Fraülein Wahlmann in August 1942; from left to right around the table are: Julius Schaub (next to the empty chair), Walter Hewel, Miss Wahlmann, a smiling Bormann, Gerhard Engel, second Bormann secretary Fraulein Fugger, and Heinrich Heim (back to camera). Bormann told Heim to secretly take down Hitler's words at mealtimes but not conferences as yet. *Puttkamer Collection, CER*

11 FHQ WOLFSSCHLUCHT 2

FHQ Wolfsschlucht 2 (W2) was a bunker complex near Margival, France. On June 5, 1940, this FHQ was ready to house Hitler closer to the Western Front for the final phase of the French campaign, but France sued for peace on June 17, making it a moot destination.

FHQ W2 became active again in 1942, as the Allies were preparing for their cross-Channel invasion of northwestern Europe. Thus, a pair of FHQs were initiated: W2 and W3. As it turned out, Hitler was present at the Margival FHQ site for only one day, on June 17, 1944. The occasion was the celebrated and stormy meeting with his two Normandy campaign managers, Army Field Marshals Gerd von Rundstedt and Erwin Rommel.

Description

W2 was situated in a deep railroad cutting that originally comprised a single concrete bunker, some wooden structures, and a tunnel to house the Führer's special train, *Brandenburg.* Later, some bomb-proof air-raid shelters and many more work bunkers were added.

The entire site covered almost fifty-six square miles. Within this area were a half dozen large bunkers and eight flat bunkers. There were also twenty barrack huts and larger, unprotected huts made of wood. There were some 450 structures in all, and antiaircraft guns ringed the entire area.

Asserted Speer in *Inside the Third Reich,* "The construction of this place cost millions for concrete and hundreds of kilometers of telephone cables." Indeed, more concrete was poured for FHQ W2 than at any other finished installation and thirteen thousand workers were used to construct it, as noted by Seidler and Ziegert. In 1944, yet a third site was being prepared at Diedenhofen in Lorraine, but Hitler did not use it.

FHQ Wolfsschlucht 2 in Action: June 17, 1944

On June 16, 1944, Hitler flew to Metz, France, and the next day he met with von Rundstedt, Rommel,

and their top staff officers in the W2 teahouse for a single, stormy, in-country summit conference concerning their losses in the Normandy campaign. Afterward they adjourned to a bunker because of the threat of an Allied air raid, and later they had lunch back in the teahouse.

The two field marshals stated the overall military situation was hopeless. When Rommel urged Hitler to make peace, the angry Führer retorted that Rommel should tend to his own front and leave the strategic direction of the war effort to him.

Hitler was supposed to visit the Desert Fox's own field headquarters just two days later but—reportedly because of an explosion of a V-rocket near the bunker—returned instead to FHQ Berghof. Wrote Max Domarus in his work *Hitler: Speeches and Proclamations,* "Several surviving military men who were with the Führer at the time deny this."

FHQ W2's Postwar Career: NATO and French Army Headquarters

As stated in *After the Battle,* in 1977,

W2 is the only former FHQ existing today where all the buildings remain intact. The bunkers at Margival were not destroyed and were taken over by American forces after the war. . . . The complex later [1955] became European North Atlantic Treaty Organization (NATO) Headquarters, with the addition of many new concrete buildings.

During 1963–69, French President Gen. Charles de Gaulle expelled NATO from France. The old W2 site remained vacant until it was occupied again in 1969, when the French Army VI Corps set up a commando-training center there. In the early 1990s, the 67th Infantry Regiment was housed in the one-time German bunkers.

The former W2 Führerbunker is today called *Marie-Aude,* while the original OKW block at Margival is now named *Marie-Jeanne.* The French Army still uses both.

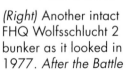

(Above) A good postwar view of the former Führerbunker, renamed and used by the French Army as *Marie-Aude. After the Battle*

(Left) FHQ W2 Building #22, a bunker near Margival, France, as it looks today. *Clayton Donnell, After the Battle*

(Left) How the former OKW W2 block at Margival appeared in 1977. *After the Battle*

(Right) Another intact FHQ Wolfsschlucht 2 bunker as it looked in 1977. *After the Battle*

# 12 FHQ ADLERHORST, 1944–1945

Hitler's FHQ Adlerhorst (Eagle's Eyrie) was located near Field Marshal Gerd von Rundstedt's own headquarters at Castle Ziegenberg, which was near Bad Nauheim in the Wetterau region of central Germany and north of Frankfurt. Hitler resided there from December 10 or 11, 1944, until January 15, 1945.

Located in a forest at the end of a sizable valley, the FHQ complex was well camouflaged. It comprised both housing and bunkers. Castle Ziegenberg, however, was never Hitler's own FHQ. According to Irwin J. Kappes in his 2003 MilitaryHistoryOnline.com article, "Hitler's Ultra-Secret *Adlerhorst*,"

> Behind the castle there was a compound made up of seven buildings giving the appearance of an innocent grouping of wooden country cottages with second-story dormers. Many even had wooden porches decorated with flower baskets. Actually, they were bunkers, and had three-foot-thick walls and ceilings of reinforced concrete . . . furnished in the bourgeois German style of the time—turned oak floor lamps with fringed shades, the obligatory deer antlers, wall hangings depicting hunting scenes or Teutonic battle scenes, knotty-pine wall paneling, and upholstered furniture designed more for appearance than for comfort.

Hitler's own dwelling was Haus (House) 1. House 2 was a casino that contained a lounge, café, situation room, and substantial communications center where the daily military conferences were held. A short, covered walkway adjoined it to House 1. OKW was located in House 3, where the top marshals and generals lived, and the second-tier generals resided in House 4. The Nazi media representatives were quartered in House 5, the Press House. House 6 was where Martin Bormann and such visiting Gauleiters as Alfred Rosenberg and Dr. Robert Ley stayed. House 7, the Wachhaus (Watch House), was the largest of the seven buildings and contained not only Hitler's offices but also the living quarters of his secretarial and housekeeping staff and personal security men.

In the village the motor pool garage was the area's largest structure. It housed the cars for Hitler and his entourage, as well as buses, fire engines, and ambulances, and served as living quarters for the families of the personnel.

From here two German offensives were launched that encompassed the Battle of the Bulge: the first—Operation Autumn Mist (or Fog)—began at 5:30 AM on December 16, 1944, in Belgium, while the second, Operation Nordwind (North Wind), began December 29 in the French province of Alsace-Lorraine. By that date, the Third Reich was at war with fifty-eight countries around the globe.

Description

FHQ Adlerhorst was the first such command facility built and the only location that Speer both designed and erected for Hitler. The Führer had rejected it in 1940 as being too grandiose for his plebeian tastes, but he used it anyway in 1945. Speer recalled how Hitler had refused to stay in the country house nearby because he felt the Castle Ziegenberg was too grand: "Something for a horse-loving aristocrat," Hitler snorted, as stated in *Inside the Third Reich*. It reminded Hitler of the castles and palatial estates favored by the disdained Kaiser Wilhelm II, and he wanted no part of that image publicly as the Führer of a working-class political party, the Nazis. Thus, Castle Ziegenberg was turned over to von Rundstedt instead.

The original Eagle's Eyrie had cost $2 million, according to Speer, and then the projected FHQ had to be relocated elsewhere for the 1940 Western campaign. But with Hitler, money was never an object.

Hitler's secretary Traudl Junge remembered in *Until the Final Hour* seeing FHQ Adlerhorst when Hitler used it during the Battle of the Bulge: "We saw the FHQ well camouflaged on one of the mountain crests. It was a beautiful place. Little log cabins clung to the wooded slopes, each of them with a deep, solid bunker underground. The rooms were small, but better furnished than at Wolf's Lair. The Führer lived in two rather larger rooms in the log cabin situated lowest down."

The field headquarters of RFSS Himmler was at nearby Kransberg, while Warlimont's Section L operational staff was with Hitler at Adlerhorst.

FHQ Adlerhorst During the Battle of the Bulge, December 1944–January 1945

What became known to the British as the "Rundstedt Offensive" and to the Americans as the Battle of the Bulge was the largest engagement ever fought by the United States Army to this day. At FHQ Adlerhorst on December 11, 1944, Hitler addressed half of his divisional commanders on the coming fight, and he met with the other half the next day.

Operation Autumn Mist started at 5:30 AM on December 16, 1944. Despite initial German victories against the Americans in the Ardennes Forest of Belgium—the very scene of his 1940 breakthrough against the British and French—the GIs hung on. When the weather cleared, Allied airpower was again felt on the ground.

Hitler gave a second pep talk to his division commanders on December 28 for the next phase of the battle, but he knew he'd already lost the last major German offensive of the war. Initially he believed that the first phase would succeed, but now he pinned his hopes instead on the second.

Noted his Luftwaffe adjutant von Below in *At Hitler's Side*,

> **The impression Hitler made on me was one of complete despair. Never before or afterwards did I see him in such a state. He now spoke of taking his own life. . . . 'I know the war is lost. The odds are too overwhelming. I have been betrayed. . . . The best thing is to put a bullet through my brain.'**

But he didn't—then.

As the Germans were losing the Battle of the Bulge, Göring told Hitler he should request an armistice from the Allies. Hitler forbade it.

Toward the end of the battle, the German High Command conferred on New Year's Day 1945 at FHQ Adlerhorst. Hitler then broke his five-month public silence with a radio broadcast. The German people had not heard from him since his July 20, 1944, address from FHQ Wolfsschanze, telling his people that he'd survived the Army Bomb Plot blast. That same day, the *New York Times* newspaper ran a story that was headlined "Nazi Chief Speaks; Tells Reich War Will Go on Into 1946 or Germany Will Win by Then."

Col. Gen. Heinz Guderian—the chief of the German General Staff since July 21, 1944—asked for more troops from the Western Front to be sent eastward on January 9. As reported in Guderian's postwar memoir, *Panzer Leader*, Hitler answered, "The Eastern Front will have to look after itself!"

Nazi Germany was fast running out of manpower to fuel its war machine. On January 12, 1945, Hitler was told at Eagle's Eyrie that the Red Army had heeded British Prime Minister Winston Churchill's request for an early Eastern Front offensive for that year to take the pressure off the Allies on the Western Front.

Now, Hitler's embattled legions were in full retreat on both fronts. He returned to FHQ New RC in Berlin on January 16 for the final phase of the lost war. Traudl Junge recalled in *Until the Final Hour*, "People were still cracking jokes. Someone said Berlin was a very practical spot for headquarters, because soon we'd be able to travel between the Eastern Front and the Western Front by suburban railway [subway]. Hitler could still laugh at that."

On April 1, 1945, Gen. George S. Patton, Jr., and the U.S. Third Army overran FHQ Adlerhorst.

Postwar Fate of FHQ Adlerhorst

The U.S. Army destroyed all five hundred of the original Amt (office) buildings after the war, except for the OKW location, upon whose foundation a hotel was built in 1957. In 1977 the West German Army began using the former hillside tunnels and caverns as storage sites, all off-limits to visitors, according to *After the Battle*.

However, as Kappes noted in his more recent article,

> **the Wachhaus . . . escaped damage and exists today. The Pressehaus also escaped demolition. . . . The two buildings are in a remarkable state of preservation. The large motor pool building . . . also went unscathed . . . converted into a military hospital in 1977 . . . and finally returned to the German government. . . . The garage itself still stands.**

The castle was a ruin for decades, but it was refurbished and made into luxury apartments in 1981. "The foundation of the OKW House has found use as the basement for the Gasthaus [Hotel] Adlerhorst."

Added Seidler and Ziegert in *Hitler's Secret Headquarters*,

> **In summer 1946, the . . . bunkers of FHQ Adlerhorst were blown up and the land was taken over by displaced persons for a settlement. In 1960, the Bundeswehr [German Federal Army] took possession of the parcel northwest of the castle and converted two former bunkers into a depot.**
>
> **The land, with the large garage east of Castle Ziegenberg, remained in US hands until 1992. In contrast to Ziegenberg, Kransberg suffered no war damage, and the castle was used as an Allied interrogation center for two years.**

Several top former Nazi leaders—as well as both industrial and technical directors—were processed through
there. Kransberg also reverted to German control, until it
was returned to private ownership in 1994.

In 2005, British author Tony LeTissier noted in *The
Third Reich: Then and Now*, "[The area] is a fashion-
able place to live. . . . All but the OKW buildings were
demolished."

(Right) View of FHQ Adlerhorst near Castle
Ziegenberg, 1939. *HHA*

(Above) One of Hitler's G-4 cross-country touring cars parked in front of a chalet at FHQ Adlerhorst,
1939. *Speer*

(Left and Above) Views of FHQ
Adlerhorst near Castle Ziegenberg,
1945. *HHA*

(Top Left) On New Year's morning 1945, the Führer received congratulations from his assembled inner circle and awarded Luftwaffe Stuka ace Col. Hans-Ulrich Rudel the unique Gold Oak Leaves with Swords and Diamonds to his Knight's Cross. From left to right are seen here: von Ribbentrop, Rudel, Fegelein, Jodl, Hitler, Keitel, Gen. Wilhelm Burgdorf, Göring, Dönitz, and Guderian. Hitler once said that he saw Rudel as a possible successor to himself as Führer, but he was probably being facetious politically. This is a previously unpublished photograph. *HHA*

(Middle Left) Another view of the scene at FHQ Adlerhorst on January 1, 1945, showing from left to right, Hitler, Speer, Jodl, Keitel and von Ribbentrop. *HHA*

(Below) A postwar view of the FHQ Adlerhorst complex. *CER*

(Top Right) High Command conference at Eagle's Eyrie on January 1, 1945, showing from left to right (front row): Göring, Hitler, unknown officer, and Guderian; back row: Luftwaffe Chief of General Staff Gen. Karl Koller (left) and SS Gen. Hermann Fegelein (right). This is another rare photo of Hitler wearing glasses. *HHA*

(Middle Right) A bunker (left) and an unidentified building (right) at FHQ Adlerhorst, as seen on March 6–7, 1945. *CER*

(Below) The aboveground section of a building at Eagle's Eyrie in early March 1945. *CER*

(Left) An American Army jeep drives through the front—though rather puny!—"security gate" of FHQ Adlerhorst on April 1, 1945. *SC*

(Left Middle) A good exterior view of a typical blockhouse-style bunker, with the aboveground portion visible here. These fortified buildings had bunkers with two underground levels and occupied almost six hundred square meters. *CER*

(Right) A postwar view of one of FHQ Adlerhorst's bunkers. *SC*

13 ZOSSEN-WÜNSDORF, 1945, AND OTHER HEADQUARTERS BUILT BUT UNUSED

On March 23, 1945, Hitler spoke with von Below and General Burgdorf at the daily military situation conference and noted that the Obersalzberg and the Berlin Führerbunker were the last real refuges that they had for command sites. He also believed that the Army headquarters at Zossen could be destroyed in one heavy air raid. General Burgdorf stated that it was still intact and that all buildings there were usable, although—as Hitler interjected—the locations of the OKH's headquarters at Maybach 1 and Maybach 2 had already been bombed once, on March 16.

At the time, some consideration was being given to relocating the Berlin FHQ to Maybach 2. According to Seidler and Ziegert in *Hitler's Secret Headquarters*, there were eleven bunker houses at Zossen's Maybach 2, with several having been set aside for Hitler as an FHQ if necessary, and Martin Bormann was strongly in favor of moving there.

From Berlin Outward

As early as March 29, 1943—when the OKW complex on Berlin's Tirpitzufer had suffered Allied bombing damage—various offices and departments had left the city for Zossen. The following June 17, 1944, Hitler directed all military staffs to exit central Berlin for that safer location.

The OKM—the Navy High Command—also left its Tirpitzufer locale by the end of 1943, transferring instead to the built-up Koralle headquarters at Bernau, northeast of the capital. The OKM moved again in March 1945 from Koralle to OKM Crocodile at Plön in Holstein and on May 2 to the Naval College at Mürwik, Dönitz's final headquarters.

Dönitz, Jodl, and Speer were all arrested by the British at the last German government site—Flensburg—on May 23, 1945. On the same date RFSS Himmler committed suicide in British custody.

OKH Maybach 1 and Maybach 2

During January 15–17, 1945, the Army command was located at the OKH Maybach 1 camp near Zossen, fifteen miles south of Berlin, while the Army General Staff was at nearby OKH Maybach 2. Both Maybach locations were named after the late popular German automobile designer, Wilhelm Maybach.

Both camps comprised stone country manor houses when viewed from outside or aerially, but each also had two-story-deep bunkers with concrete roofs underground. Both Maybachs 1 and 2 had been built during 1938–40, about a kilometer away from each other. Maybach 1 was under the jurisdiction of the General Staff, while Maybach 2 came under the Army Transportation Command.

Zeppelin and Amt (Office) 500

Besides the Army High Command and General Staff (whose field headquarters was initially code-named Zeppelin, after the famed dirigible genius Count Ferdinand Zeppelin), Zossen also housed Amt (Office) 500, the largest long-distance central communications system in the entire Reich.

Noted Hugh Thomas in *The Murder of Adolf Hitler*, "Hitler grunted. What did he need telephone communications for at this late date? More important, he had no intention of dying in an unknown hamlet. He wanted a superlative stage when the final curtain came down, and there was no better stage than a flaming Berlin," the former capital of his military hero, Frederick the Great of Prussia.

Why Not FHQ Zossen?

The four-story bunker blockhouses at Zossen resembled normal housing from their exteriors—with slanted, pointed roofs—but inside were two fortified floors above ground and two more below. All were connected by underground passageways as well.

Indeed, such facilities had always been reserved for Hitler at Zossen, but he refused to occupy them. First, he didn't feel that it was secure enough. Hitler also feared such a move, coming only months after the Army Bomb Plot explosion, would lead to his being kidnapped by his own generals for political purposes if he was permanently among them. He also preferred summoning his commanders to him as he wished, instead of he going to them. Even Keitel and Jodl did not have quarters in the Berlin FHQ Führerbunker. They traveled daily back and forth to their separate villas in the formerly posh Berlin suburb of Dahlem; so did Gen. Hans Krebs, last chief of the General Staff, from Zossen.

This travel caused great problems for the German High Command, as daily three-way trips—Zossen, Dahlem, and central Berlin—had to be made for all to be present at FHQ Führerbunker briefings.

In addition, Dr. Thomas in *The Murder of Adolf Hitler* noted, "Hitler rightly feared that the inclusion of his own little circle of sycophants into a vast Army command bunker would dangerously expose his own physical state to ridicule, and his mental status and decisions to question."

Instead, Hitler opted for a permanent division. "And separation there certainly was: one small switchboard, one radio and one radio-telephone were the sum total of Hitler's links from FHQ Führerbunker Berlin to the outside military reality," wrote Thomas.

"By choosing to remain in the Bunker, Hitler was deliberately abdicating responsibility for the conduct of the war—a fact that didn't pass unnoticed by the OKH, although it seems to have escaped historians."

The Berlin FHQ Führerbunker Versus Zossen

Hugh Thomas continued:

The Berlin Bunker contrasted sharply with the OKH headquarters at Zossen, where a bunker complex at least seven times larger than the Berlin system had a central switchboard—possibly the largest in Europe—connecting it with all parts of the Nazi empire, directly linked and servicing the combined General Staff.

Zossen would have been the obvious place to be if Hitler had really wished to continue the war, but Hitler wished instead to continue the facade of war. His Berlin Bunker wasn't even on a direct line to the Zossen headquarters; it was served by a hastily installed switchboard, effectively completed by Siemens in November 1944, which was about the size one would nowadays expect to find in a sleazy hotel.

The Fall of Zossen and OKH Maybach 1 and Maybach 2

Both Maybachs 1 and 2 fell to the Soviet Third Guards Tank Army on Hitler's fifty-sixth and last birthday, April 20, 1945, while he remained safe and sound in the Berlin FHQ Führerbunker another ten days. Perhaps he made the right choice after all!

The Berlin-Zossen-Wünsdorf-Juterbog complex remained in Russian—as opposed to Communist East German—hands until 1994, almost fifty years after the fall of the Third Reich. The complex served as the active headquarters of the Soviet Fighting Forces Group Germany, and the facilities were still usable because they were only slightly damaged by the retreating Germans in 1945.

Other Headquarters, Built but Unused

Even during all the time that Hitler spent away from Berlin in his various active field FHQs, building was constant in the preparation of ever-vaster FHQs; however, they were never used. Construction on these sites continued up to the very last week of the war, seemingly echoing Hitler's oft-stated prediction that the fighting would last until the year 1950.

Anlage Süd (Camp South) and Camp Mitte (Center)

Even as Wolfsschanze was being completed, two other possible FHQ locations were simultaneously under construction prior to the start of the Russian campaign on June 22, 1941: Anlage Mitte (Camp Center) was near Tomaszow, southeast of Lodz in central Poland, while Anlage Süd (Camp South) was located north of a rail line between Strzyzow and Frysztak and west of Przemysl in southeastern Poland. Work at Süd continued into 1944, just as at Wolfsschanze.

Hitler never even visited Camp Center, but he and the Duce stayed overnight at FHQ Anlage Süd on August 27, 1941. The German High Command regarded both locations as suitable alternate FHQs if the early stage of the Eastern Front campaign took a turn for the worse.

Indeed, even Hitler expressed this view, since on the very day the invasion started Red Army units were less than sixty-three miles from Wolfsschanze, at Bialystok. Given his later evident disdain for the unhealthy climate at Wolfsschanze, why he never abandoned it for the other locales available to him is a mystery.

Alternative FHQs, 1941–44

By 1944 several FHQs were in operation, ready, and waiting as needed: Wolfsschanze; Berghof; even the former FHQ Felsennest, then code-named Anlage Falke (Camp Falcon); and Anlage WO at Rodert, southwest of Cologne.

Meanwhile, W2 at Margival, France, had been given to Army Group B, which was trying to stop the Allied advance from Normandy. Brunhilde was being readied near Diedenhofen (or Thionville) in Lorraine in northeastern France, but as General Patton's Third Army came near, it too was evacuated before it could be used as an FHQ.

Partially usable was Camp Siegfried/Hagan at Pullach, south of Munich, while construction had also begun on Anlagens Lothar, Wolfsburg (Wolf's Storm), Wolfsberg

(Wolf's Mountain), and Olga, near Ohrdruf in the foothills of the Thuringian Forest to the west of Erfurt.

In addition, construction of Rüdiger was well under way west of Breslau in Silesia. This enormous complex included Anlage Riese (Camp Giant), near Bad Charlottenbrunn, which was destined for both Hitler and the OKW, while the OKH would get still another at Hirschberg. Once completed, FHQ Riese would have been the largest FHQ ever.

Money and Labor Cost

By September 1944, at least $60 million had been spent on unnecessary and unused headquarters, and Hitler never even visited these building sites. Altogether, some twenty-eight thousand workers had been employed as well. Camp Siegfried/Hagen was appropriated with 13 million RM and Anlage Riese had been granted 150 million RM, but neither were ever ready for occupancy.

Hitler's Bunker Mania

Hitler had been interested in bunker construction since his combat days in World War I, but with the start of his own war in 1939, it became an all-consuming mania with him. Indeed, he became intimately involved with such minute details as the thickness of ceilings and how to correctly insulate concrete layering. As Allied bombers began using maximum-weight 10,000-kilogram bombs by the end of 1944, Hitler ordered again and again that the ceilings in both military and civilian air-raid shelters be increased in thicknesses.

Riese, the Imperial FHQ

On June 20, 1944, Speer reported to Hitler on the plans for FHQ Riese at Castle Furstenstein. Taken over by the Reich in 1940, the castle had originally been the ancestral home of the princes of Pless. Work would be hurried to make it ready for occupancy by November 1, 1944; however, its living areas and bomb shelters would not be ready until August 1945.

Apparently, no one realized it was one of the Kaiser's own supreme headquarters from World War I, something that Hitler would not like. That this headquarters was on the site of a royal castle meant that Hitler was likely to veto it even when it was finished, as he had done with Castle Ziegenberg. Nevertheless, construction continued apace.

Incredibly, Hitler's suite was to comprise both the tapestry and Italian rooms of the castle—plus several more rooms to entertain guests of state—with an elevator to the below-ground bunkers. Dining would take place in the Crooked Hall, while his entourage would be fed in the Imperial Rooms. An outside entry to the underground bunkers was off of the castle's terrace.

Not only would Reich Marshal Göring have a suite of four rooms, but there would also be a trio of apartments and twenty individual rooms for Hitler's closest aides. The family of his housekeeper, Artur Kannenberg, would also be housed there.

By the end of 1944—as the war was being lost on all fronts—fully twenty-three thousand workers were building the future, grandiose FHQ Riese. Indeed, more than twice the concrete used at Wolfsschanze was needed for the project. Even as the Red Army approached its Silesian environs, workers were still finishing the below-ground bunkers, and work was finally stopped only a few days before the enemy occupied Riese in May 1945.

S-3: A Secret SS FHQ?

Late in June 1944, construction of Site S-3 began in Thuringia's Harz Mountains, but it was never completed. Hitler had apparently authorized this new building project, although Speer was unaware of it. It may even have been a secret SS FHQ, as Himmler's chief of construction—Hans Kammler—was in charge and not Speer's own OT, which was occupied building FHQ Riese. Supposedly, the RFSS planned to present Hitler with FHQ S-3 as a birthday gift, but it is also possible that Himmler planned to use it himself as Germany's first SS Führer had he taken over in a coup.

To this day, no one knows for sure the real purpose of S-3, and thus it remains one of the unsolved mysteries of the war.

FHQs Everlasting . . .

Bizarrely, even in the final weeks of the lost war, Speer's OT was still seeking future FHQ location sites in central Germany as well as on its Austrian border. As late as April 8, 1945—only a month before the German surrender—eight such locales were reported in a secret OT memo. While half of these were rejected, and the other four underground bunker complexes—Bad Berka, Ebensee, Niedersachswerfen, and Lothar on the Obersalzberg—were considered usable, none were ever employed. Still, OT trial drillings and land surveys continued in the Tyrol and at Salzkammergut.

The OT FHQ construction mania finally ended when the Germans ran out of time and building materials and when the enemy arrived on the doorstep.

Falling FHQ Dominos, 1945–2006

The U.S. Army occupied Martin Bormann's planned Nazi Party FHQ, Siegfried/Hagen in Pullach in late April 1945. A special commission reviewed what had been completed and stated that the Pullach location outside Munich was safe, modern, and a first-class facility. It is still used to this day by the German military.

The final headquarters for Keitel and Jodl was at the Army's Cavalry School barracks at Krampnitz near Potsdam. On the night of April 24, 1945, they prepared to move to OKW North between Rheinsburg and Fürstenburg, with Keitel assuming its command on Hitler's agreement—his first such charge of the entire war.

That same night, Jodl virtually wiped out the OKH by having Hitler sign an order putting the Führer in charge of just three organizations: OKW, OKM, and the Luftwaffe. Neither Keitel nor Jodl ever saw Hitler again, after more than two thousand days at war together.

German Army and a single Luftwaffe (center) staff officer on parade at Zossen in 1939. *HHA*

14 VORBUNKER AND FHQ FÜHRERBUNKER

itler's thirteenth and final command center of World War II was the famous FHQ Führerbunker under the Old RC–New RC complex in Berlin. Many myths and legends have been created over the years about this most famous of all FHQs, and herein I shall set the record straight.

Why Did Hitler Stay in Berlin at All?

Most recent historians have raised the valid question of why Hitler chose Berlin for his final FHQ. After all, he could have gone to Prague, where there were strong German SS forces to command, or to Norway, where the German Army and Navy were present in strength as well. But he felt that, in the end, he would face the same choice there as in Berlin: victory or death. If death it was to be, then his capital was the best place for it.

If he left his capital city of Berlin, as the Kaiser did in 1918, Hitler felt that he would disappear from the stage of world history as a dishonored runaway. He had also seen how his enemy Stalin had courageously refused to desert Moscow under very similar circumstances in 1941. If Stalin could summon forth a victory then, so could he in 1945. Also, Hitler's admiration for his hero, Frederick the Great, included the knowledge that the Russians of that day had occupied Berlin (as had the French in 1806), and the Prussians had still won their respective wars both times in the end. So would he, he believed.

According to von Below in *At Hitler's Side*, Hitler dreaded an American occupation of the capital even more than that of the Red Army because he feared the power of the Jews of the United States more than he did that of the Bolsheviks. He had also signed one pact with Stalin in 1939 and was perfectly prepared to do so again, just as the Western Allies always feared. In 1945, however, Stalin no longer needed him.

Thus, it was from the underground Führerbunker that Hitler made his last radio appeal to his people, met with his Gauleiters in a final session on February 25, and departed from there on Sunday, March 3, 1945, on his last visit to the Eastern Front, then at the Oder River. This last visit took place on Heroes' Memorial Day as Göring, Keitel, and Dönitz reviewed troops in Berlin in his place. Hitler

traveled thirty miles northeast of Berlin by road to Harnekop Castle at Bad Freienwalde, where he met with Gen. Theodor Busse, then commander of the Ninth Army, at his field headquarters to discuss defensive plans. Afterward he returned to FHQ New RC Berlin for good.

He rejected Bormann's entreaties to go to FHQ Lothar, the alpine redoubt on the Obersalzberg, for the following reasons (as detailed by Anton Joachimsthaler in *The Last Days of Hitler*):

> **I am the Führer as long as I can still lead. I cannot lead by going away and sitting on a mountain somewhere, but only if I have the authority over armies that obey me. In the south, I would have neither army nor influence.**

In addition to refusing to leave Berlin, Hitler rejected the idea of surrendering to the enemy. Adamantly, he turned down Baur's repeated offers to fly him to Japan, Argentina, or one of the Arab states, where he might have continued his race war against the Jews from the Mideast.

The Vorbunker (Front Bunker)

During 1935–36, a reinforced cellar was built beneath the Old RC Diplomats' Hall at the rear of the building. This air-raid shelter was the first of a series beneath the growing complex. It covered six thousand square feet, but the usable area in the interior was only 2,230 square feet, with inner walls that were eighteen inches thick and ten feet high from floor to ceiling.

This bunker had narrow rooms with a central corridor of connecting doors, beginning with a hallway and a storage room. Next came a central dining room, and then a passageway leading down—later on—to the Führerbunker. On one side of the central corridor were toilets, showers, a kitchen, and an apartment of three rooms—later occupied by Frau Göbbels and her six children—while on the opposite side was the FBK/RSD police guardroom.

The accommodations in both the Vorbunker and the later Führerbunker were hot, poorly ventilated, and very cramped. During the later daily military situation conferences,

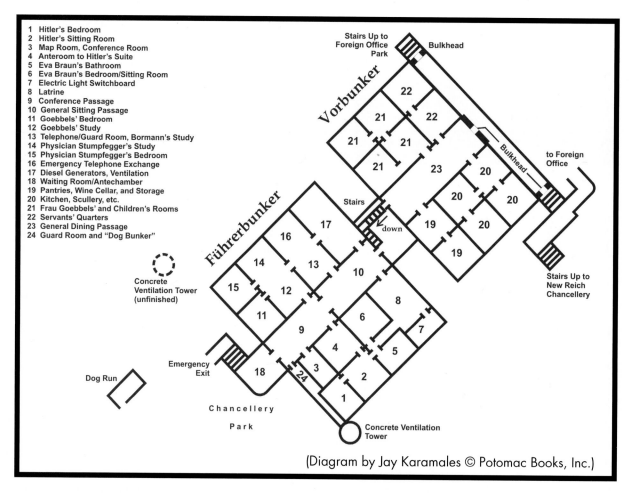

1 Hitler's Bedroom
2 Hitler's Sitting Room
3 Map Room, Conference Room
4 Anteroom to Hitler's Suite
5 Eva Braun's Bathroom
6 Eva Braun's Bedroom/Sitting Room
7 Electric Light Switchboard
8 Latrine
9 Conference Passage
10 General Sitting Passage
11 Goebbels' Bedroom
12 Goebbels' Study
13 Telephone/Guard Room, Bormann's Study
14 Physician Stumpfegger's Study
15 Physician Stumpfegger's Bedroom
16 Emergency Telephone Exchange
17 Diesel Generators, Ventilation
18 Waiting Room/Antechamber
19 Pantries, Wine Cellar, and Storage
20 Kitchen, Scullery, etc.
21 Frau Goebbels' and Children's Rooms
22 Servants' Quarters
23 General Dining Passage
24 Guard Room and "Dog Bunker"

(Diagram by Jay Karamales © Potomac Books, Inc.)

Hitler would order the diesel machinery needed to run the two bunkers' pumping system and ventilation to be turned off because of the noise it made. Then his guests would complain of headaches because it became so stuffy.

During 1943–44, Allied bombing attacks on Berlin increased in both tempo and severity. As a result, on January 18, 1943, Hitler ordered that a second, stronger bunker—deeper down into the earth and with a thicker roof—should be built. Thus was born the concept of the later, more famous FHQ Führerbunker, well known to all students of Hitler's last days.

According to Joachimsthaler, Hitler told its architect, Speer,

> Since the air raid shelter in the Old RC only has a ceiling 1.6 meters thick, a bunker must immediately be built . . . according to the new dimensions [ceiling 3.5 meters and sides 3.5–4 meters thick], but with the same internal dimensions as the existing bunker. [Carl] Piepenburg is to supervise the construction.

Speer submitted his first designs to Hitler on February 6–7, 1943, just a week after the catastrophic surrender of the German Sixth Army at Stalingrad that was the turning point of the war in the east. Hitler approved the designs but wanted thicker walls and roofs, and work commenced in April 1944.

> A pit approximately 10 meters deep was dug. The outer wall of the banqueting hall on the park side was pierced at the floor level of the old air raid shelter and 1.2 meter thick reinforced concrete walls were erected to form a protected passage leading from the emergency exit of the old shelter to the outer wall of the new shelter.

Built alongside the earlier Vorbunker, the Führerbunker was to encompass a space measuring 3,350 square feet, providing a larger working area. To connect the two—the higher Vorbunker with the lower Führerbunker—there was an angled staircase.

The Führerbunker

Bunker #B207 would not be completed until early 1945. It was never intended to be an actual permanent FHQ, so the underground structure was a temporary air-raid shelter—a partially above-ground building—and not a bunker at all. Nevertheless, both buildings came to be referred to as bunkers, so I shall continue that trend here for simplicity's sake.

Settled deep into the notoriously sandy and marshy soil of Berlin, the bunker's foundations were made of specialized concrete two meters (2.19 yards) thick. The entire single-block, boxlike construction sat on a concrete drainage pan that allowed the water runoff to be pumped out mechanically.

Work progressed on the new Führerbunker right up until the time of Hitler's return from FHQ Adlerhorst on January 16, 1945, after the Battle of the Bulge.

The Führerbunker had three entrances, all with steel doors that were gas-proofed. The most commonly used entrance was gained through the tunnel system from the original Vorbunker. The entryway from the Vorbunker was a concrete stairway that led down in right-angle turns to the empty passage that went into the Führerbunker itself.

The rooms of the bunker were roughly thirty feet underground and had nine-foot ceilings overhead. Angled steel girders supported the walls, per Hitler's orders. He also ordered that the ceiling of the Führerbunker be overlaid with a buried steel mesh and, on top of that, granite slabs to detonate Allied bombs at the level of the surface instead of having them penetrate the ceiling and blow up the bunker from within.

Entirely self-sufficient, the bunker's lighting, water pumps, small kitchen, toilets, washroom, heating, and ventilation were all supplied with electricity generated by its own diesel engine. A central hallway divided the entire structure.

When Did Hitler and Eva Braun Move into the Führerbunker?

From his return to Berlin from the Western Front on January 16 through March 15, 1945, Hitler lived and worked in FHQ Old RC. Then he descended into the Führerbunker for good on March 15 because of constant Allied air raids, despite the fact that it was not yet fully ready for him. There were ventilation problems and even some flooding in the upper Vorbunker from the area's high water table. Prior to March 15 he did take shelter in the Führerbunker from Allied air raids, and after he took up permanent residency there, Hitler still surfaced periodically for air and walking his dog, Blondi.

At the same time—mid-March 1945—Eva Braun arrived in Berlin for the last time to stay in the Old RC. She descended below on April 15, 1945, a month after Hitler did, and she remained there with him until their deaths together fifteen days later on April 30, 1945. Oddly, no photographs by photographer Eva Braun Hitler have ever appeared from this period and place.

In all, Hitler used the fabled Führerbunker—perhaps the best-known command center in all military history—for a total of 105 days. They have been chronicled in books, movies, documentaries, and even television miniseries, the stars of which portray Hitler, Eva, Speer, Bormann, and the Göbbels family.

Living Conditions: "A Cement Submarine"

Every explosion above and outside the Führerbunker brought down dust inside, made talk impossible, and scared all the occupants. Hitler especially feared that a direct hit might crack the FHQ's outer shell, and they would drown in the high water table.

The interior painting was never finished and black mold grew on the inside walls and ceilings, while water leaked into the generator room and had to be mopped three times a day. Also, conditions were close, and human body odor soon became a real irritant. The sewers stopped up and all the toilets became blocked as well, with only Eva's being at all usable. Blondi delivered eight puppies in March and these were placed in the latrine area. Later, all were murdered on Hitler's orders.

Drinking sessions among the soldiers became commonplace in the Vorbunker, then later on down below, with heavy clouds of cigarette smoke drifting above. Hitler no longer seemed to care, or his distaste for smoking was ignored.

Said SS Capt. Helmut Beermann, in *The Murder of Adolf Hitler*,

> The whole atmosphere down there was . . . like being stranded in a cement submarine, or buried alive in some charnel house. People who work in diving bells probably feel less cramped. It was dank and dusty. . . . The ventilation could be now warm and sultry, now cold and clammy. . . . Then there [were] the fetid odors of boots, sweaty woolen uniforms, and acrid coal-tar disinfectant. Towards the end, when the drainage packed in, it was as pleasant as working in a public urinal.

Daily Briefings

On March 13, 1948, Maj. Bernd Freytag von Loringhoven testified the following at the first Nuremberg trial:

> At first, the briefings were held daily in Berlin in the New or Old Chancellery . . . but during the final weeks, they took place down inside the *Führerbunker* in a very, very small room. On account of the air raids, there was often not enough time to bring all the maps, etc., down into the Bunker. That is why the briefings were finally [all] held in the Bunker.

The conference room measured about ten by thirteen feet, with a bench along a wall, a few chairs, a table for the maps, and a lamp. As was his usual custom, Hitler alone sat while everyone else stood around him at the map table; however, according to von Loringhoven in the Nuremberg testament documents, "the older officers who attended the daily briefings could sit on the chairs from time to time, because the briefings often lasted for hours."

With sometimes as many as eighteen to twenty people in the small room, the air quickly grew oppressive, and concentration became extremely difficult. There was a bookcase along the wall that contained only paper, pencils, and other office material, and the room was lit by a single hanging bulb in its center, a far cry from the ornate rooms of the New Reich Chancellery or the well-equipped Wolfsschanze of old. Such was Hitler's final direction of World War II, from a small space to a global conflict and vice versa.

Communications

Besides the antiquated Führerbunker telephone switchboard, there was one medium- and long-range German Army radio transmitter, with an outdoor aerial hanging from a balloon that provided a capability of radio-telephone communication, but it was highly vulnerable to Russian artillery fire (it was knocked out twice). The FHQ's links to the outside world also consisted of messengers on foot, car, or motorcycle.

With the fall of OKH HQ Zossen, Berlin was effectively cut off by telephone to outside Wehrmacht units altogether. Incredibly, sometime during April 22–23, 1945, the Army's signals unit simply left the Chancellery, resulting in total chaos. Beyond Hitler's map room, there was only SS Sgt. Rochus Misch at his simple switchboard—an unbelievable situation for anyone attempting to direct a modern war! Still, Martin Bormann's secretary also maintained the Nazi Party's telex system, which was totally separate from the military's direction of the war effort.

As the Red Army stormed into the Berlin suburbs, Hitler's staff officers found themselves sitting next to Sergeant Misch as he called old friends in various parts of the city to ask if they had seen any Soviet tanks lately. Finally, for the entire final week of World War II, the telephone switchboard of FHQ Führerbunker Berlin was effectively dead, although Joachimsthaler said some telephone calls were made until April 29, the day before Hitler's death.

Thus, Hitler became dependent on the British Broadcasting Corporation (BBC) radio broadcasts for the information to formulate his final grand strategic designs of World War II. It was also through this forbidden medium that he learned on April 29 of RFSS Himmler's treachery: he had opened secret surrender negotiations with the enemy via neutral Sweden.

As radio contact became ever more unreliable in the final days, couriers had to be used instead. Couriers carried the three copies of Hitler's last will and testament to the outside world. General Burgdorf sent Maj. Willy Johannmeier on foot to deliver a copy to Field Marshal Schörner. Bormann sent his aide, SS Col. Wilhelm Zander, to Grand Admiral Dönitz with another. The third was forwarded to the Brown House in Munich by Dr. Göbbels.

Then, around 12:50 PM on April 29, 1945, the radio was gone for good, when the balloon was destroyed during an Allied air raid. "Doubtless this factor, too, was one of the many that the besieged Führer considered when he decided to kill himself 26 hours later at 3:30 PM on the 30th," concluded Joachimsthaler.

The Reich Split Asunder

On April 15, 1945, to prepare for the splitting of Nazi Germany by the invading Allied armies from both fronts, Hitler designated two new, domestic regional military commanders under himself at Berlin. Luftwaffe Field Marshal Albert Kesselring would command the southern half of the Third Reich, while Grand Admiral Dönitz would reign supreme in the north.

Thus, in the last two weeks of the war, an Air Force officer and a Navy sailor commanded Germany's ground forces. In the end, the former surrendered to the Americans and the latter to the British.

The Führer in Decline

And what of Hitler himself? He suffered either an actual or feigned nervous breakdown on April 22, 1945, declaring that the war was lost and that he'd been betrayed—which was true enough in both cases. Nevertheless, Hitler either acted out this scene of purple-faced rage with screaming, fist pounding, and arm waving, or else he pulled himself together enough for the last eight days of his life and died cool, calm, and collected, if all eyewitness accounts are to be believed. On April 23, Hitler was in conference with Speer when the famous Göring telegram arrived that asked if the Reich Marshal could take over the government if Hitler, trapped in Berlin, was no longer able to function; it was not a coup attempt, as Martin Bormann alleged. Hitler fired Göring from all his posts but never ordered his death just in case he might need his faithful paladin later.

Recalled von Loringhoven later at Nuremberg,

Most of the people had nothing left to do there. . . . They saw themselves as living corpses, and spent the final days in their rooms. . . . A major topic in all the conversations was when and how one was supposed to kill oneself. . . .

And yet, in the end, few actually did.

What Happened to the Painting of Frederick the Great?

By all accounts of the last days in FHQ Führerbunker, at Hitler's farewell meeting with pilot Hans Baur on April 30, 1945, he presented Baur with a present: the famous small oval portrait of King Frederick the Great of Prussia by Adolf Menzel, which had traveled across the Third Reich and German-occupied Europe to all of Hitler's various FHQs throughout the war.

According to Max Domarus in *Hitler: Speeches and Proclamations,*

> **Baur rolled up the portrait and carried it with him in his knapsack as he left the Bunker on the night of May 1, 1945. His escape was cut short, since he was wounded the next day and fell into the hands of Russian soldiers. Since he was incapable of providing any other information on the fate of the painting, it is highly likely that it was lost while Baur was fleeing from the Chancellery and was destroyed in the general confusion.**

My own view is Baur either threw it away or destroyed it himself to prevent it from falling to the Red Army, or it was taken from him by the soldiers and, after his release a decade later, he was ashamed to admit either event, as it had been personally entrusted to him by his still-beloved Führer. In either case, though, the Russians have never said that they had it. Perhaps it will yet turn up someday.

Death of the Hitlers

Hitler issued his last order to Gen. Helmuth Weidling at 3:00 PM on April 30, 1945, exactly one half hour before his death. As both the expected and ordered relief expeditions of Army Gen. Walther Wenck and SS General Steiner had failed to relieve the capital, Hitler ordered:

> **To the Commander of the defense of Berlin. . . . In the event of ammunition and supplies to the defenders of the capital being in danger of running out, I give my permission for a breakout . . . to take place in small groups, which are to attempt a link-up with forces still fighting elsewhere. Where this is not successful, the fight is to continue in the forests. Adolf Hitler.**

A similar order was sent to Reich Chancellery Combat Commandant SS Gen. Wilhelm Mohnke as well, also at 3:00 PM the same day. Thus the Army and SS were for once treated just the same by Hitler.

Hitler received General Mohnke, the final commander of the one thousand–man guard regiment defending the Old RC–New RC complex on April 30. Mohnke told

Hitler (who was clad in bathrobe, pajamas, and slippers) on April 30 that some Red Army troops were even then alongside the New RC on the Voss Strasse side of the structure. He expected the final Soviet assault to come the next morning—May 1, 1945—to celebrate the taking of Berlin on the Communist Party May Day, or the international workers' holiday.

One of modern political, social, and military history's greatest gamblers concluded that he had effectively run out of time at last. That same day, he and his new bride of just thirty-nine hours killed themselves together: he with a single pistol shot to the right temple and she with a cyanide poison capsule.

Their dead bodies were carried out of the Führerbunker through its upper exit into the debris-scattered and bomb-blasted Reich Chancellery park, then burned, and partially buried on the grounds of the final wartime FHQ—right where it had all started on September 1, 1939.

The war lasted only a week longer. The Allies accepted the Germans' surrender in the west from Jodl on May 7, and the Russians in the east from Keitel on May 8.

The Red Army Arrives

On Tuesday, May 1, 1945, the Red Army 284th and the 230th Rifle Divisions began their final assault on the buildings facing the Reich Chancellery complex. That night, at 11:00 PM, the first breakout party from FHQ Führerbunker under General Mohnke's command obeyed Hitler's last order and tried to escape from Berlin, followed by others. There our saga ends.

Postwar

In June 1945, groundwater began seeping into and then flooding the former Führerbunker. By 1947, both of the outside observation towers and the small concrete exit bunker were in ruins, but the stairwell going down remained. From February 21, 1949, the systematic demolition of the entire complex of buildings and underground shelters by sections was attempted. However, the Führerbunker—despite the size of the charges used—could not be completely destroyed. Some of the debris was trucked off for use in construction. The Soviets used some of the debris along with the precious red marble from the interior of the New Reich Chancellery to build both the Russian Memorial in Berlin-Treptow and as the new Kaiserhof underground subway station, where it can still be seen to this day.

The area of the former Führerbunker was covered over with dirt, but still quite a visible mound marked the spot. For years its location was in a no-man's-land in East Berlin, a little more than a thousand feet from the notorious Berlin Wall. By 1988 the mound was removed, the remains of the twin observation towers were trucked away at last, and later, bit by bit, the remaining hole was finally filled in with dirt. Later on, built over the top of all this was a road and apartment buildings for workers, perhaps a fitting memorial after all to a road builder who was also the leader of the National Socialist German Workers' Party.

(Right) A superb aerial view of the ground immediately above both the Vorbunker and FHQ Führerbunker in 1945, showing the observation pillbox or tower at lower left (conical turret roof), and next to it above the one-story emergency exit, with the unfinished pillbox tower at its upper left corner. Note, too, the smaller ventilation tower at the center top of the photo, just under the tall tree; through it, as he testified at Nuremberg, Speer allegedly wanted to poison all the Führerbunker residents but failed. The Hitlers were burned just opposite of the pillbox's exit/entryway (left of the actual building). The Vorbunker was under the structure at far right, while the Führerbunker was underneath the open square formed in the middle, including the two towers and exit at far left. *LC*

(Right) Here is one of the few photographs taken in the Führerbunker prior to May 2, 1945. This is either the waiting room or, according to *After the Battle*, the corridor outside the Führerbunker proper. From left to right are: Dr. Morell (face turned away); two RSD guards (with a third obscured); SS man Karl Wilhelm Krause, Hitler's former valet; Adm. Karl-Jesko von Puttkamer; and two more RSD men. Note, too, the leather coat hanging on the wall at right, perhaps a clue that this was the corridor. *LC*

(Below) A Soviet photo of the interior of the bunker, also rare. LC

(Above) The passageway or corridor inside the actual Führerbunker, immediately after the war in 1945—a rare view. Beneath the Chancellery park, architect Carl Piepenburg and the Hochtief construction firm began preparing the Führerbunker site in 1943. The cost was 1,353,460.16 RM. When Hitler occupied it, the concrete was still wet, with cables and water pipes everywhere—a mere one hundred yards away from the Chancellor's Old RC luxurious apartment. The Führerbunker's foundation was almost forty feet deep, and the almost twelve-foot-thick roof was nearly seven feet below ground. Every time the surrounding area was either bombed or shelled, the bunkers shook in Berlin's sandy soil. SC

(Right) According to After the Battle, "one of the last people to leave the Führerbunker was SS Capt. Günther Schwaggermann, Dr. Goebbels' [sic] adjutant. Taking the last jerry can, he doused the refreshment room [seen here] with gas, tossed a flaming rag inside and quickly shut the door." On the left (out of the frame) was the room with the couch on which the Hitlers had committed suicide the day before. SC

(Right) This is the only known picture of Hitler in the Führerbunker, probably taken in the reception room, according to *After the Battle*. At left is Army Field Marshal Ferdinand Schörner (promoted April 5, 1945), who attended the afternoon situation conference with Hitler on April 21. On the thirtieth—his last day alive—Hitler named him head of the by-then nonexistent Wehrmacht. At right, Schaub looks on. It is this author's belief that this occasion is that of

Schörner's appointment as the last field marshal of the German Army, and he is being congratulated by the Führer on April 5, 1945; [but the date may be April 21, 1945]. This is the only known Heinrich Hoffmann photo from inside the Führerbunker ever to surface . *HHA*

(Above) Hitler's last military review, of Hitler Youth boys in the New RC park, in front of the wall outside his office. Left to right: Gen. Hans Krebs, the young defenders of Berlin, Artur Axmann, Hitler, and SS General Fegelein—Himmler's liaison officer—in his last public appearance before the German newsreel cameraman. Hitler had him shot for desertion in another part of the park on the night of April 28–29, 1945. *HHA*

(Above) A 1947–48 Russian Kukryniksy Collective painting titled *The End: The Last Days of Hitler's HQ in the Underground Reich's Office*, complete with distraught a Hitler, drunken Army general (center), SS officers (right), a flag-draped conference table, and even a Speer-designed chair from the New RC Cabinet Room—great postwar Soviet propaganda imagery at its best! The trio of artists who produced this epic painting was Mikhail Kupriyanov, Nikolai Sokolov, and Porfiry Krylov. It hangs in the Tretyakov Gallery. *LC*

(Left) A Red Army soldier sits on a couch in the Führerbunker conference room, where the Hitlers were married on April 29, 1945. Note that he has his boots planted on a sofa cushion to keep them away from the water that seeped into the bunker. *LC*

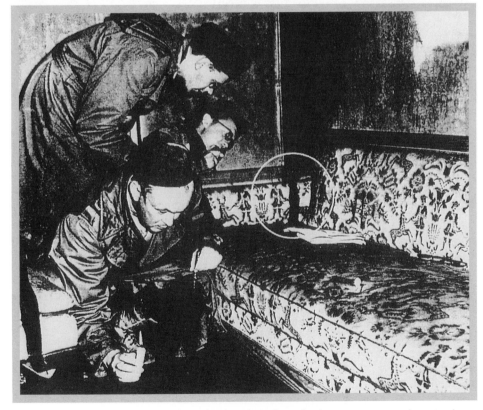

(Below left) American Army war correspondents survey the couch on which Hitler died, including his blood on the armrest at left (circled). Noted Traudl Junge in her postwar study *Until the Final Hour,* "When an incendiary bomb made the living rooms above uninhabitable, particularly the library, it [the Führerbunker] became permanent living space for Hitler and his staff. The adjutant's wing—as it was called—which contained the little Staircase Room, had not been damaged. This was where we had our typewriters and did our office work, and now we ate lunch there with Hitler, too, but in the evening, punctual as clockwork, enemy aircraft came over, and we had to dine with Hitler in the little room in the Bunker where he lived and worked. It was a tiny place in the very heart of the new Führerbunker. Then came the section of corridor leading to Hitler's rooms. It was also used as a waiting room and sitting room. . . . Next to Hitler's bedroom, there was another small room that was used for conferences, talks and military briefings." *Signal Corps*

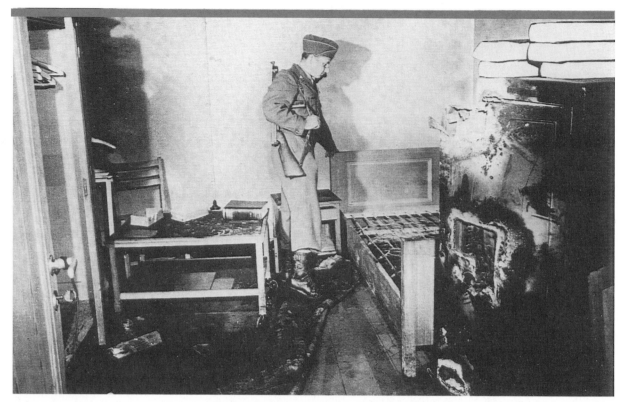

(Above) Hitler's bedroom. Of his office/living room, recalled secretary Christa Schröder in *Hitler Was My Boss,* "when someone walked through the room, the chairs had to be moved" because it was so small. Thus Hitler—the man who'd begun his career in shabby little rooms in Munich—now had come full circle, from the grandeur of Speer's New RC to the tiny hovel in which he ended his life. The safe (right) was cut open by the Russians, but Schaub had already burned most of its contents on Hitler's orders. The book on the end table at left may well be the later controversial "Linge diary" (his appointment or schedule book, really), which remained in that exact spot for some months after the war. The GI in the photo is Pvt. Peter Saltz of Brooklyn, New York. *Signal Corps*

(Right) Originally, this picture was identified as that of a young Red Army senior sergeant pointing to the spot where Eva Braun Hitler sat when she poisoned herself. However, after comparing this photo to the

previous one, this author has concluded that the soldier is sitting instead
on Hitler's bed. He is even resting his
arm on the same book seen in the
prior photo on the table behind the
GI. The subsequent Soviet autopsy
commission ruled that neither Hitler
nor Eva died of any gunshot wounds,
but from poison instead. Initially, I was
inclined to agree, but there was the
mystery of the blood on the armrest of
the sofa. This, too, was cleared up in
the 2005 publication of the Russian
report to Stalin, *The Hitler Book.* The
current opinion is that Hitler shot
himself in the right temple with his
pistol, just as all the Führerbunker
residents had always maintained. *LC*

(Below left) The outside of the left armrest on Hitler's side of the death sofa, with a stripped-away portion showing, most likely, his blood from a head shot (circled top and bottom). Since the Soviets still have the couch, presumably in Moscow, it would be a simple matter to do a DNA sample of that blood today and compare it with a known living Hitler relative, of which there are several. That is how the bodies of Russian Tsar Nicholas II, his wife, and most of their children were identified in the USSR when their bodies were exhumed. *LC*

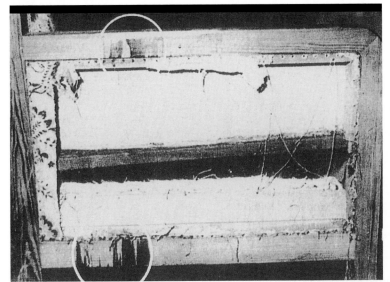

(Below) Taken in October 1945, this is a delegation from the U.S. Secretary of the Interior's Office. From left to right are: Alton Jones, S. Richardson, Robert E. Hardwick, and Joseph P. Zook. Note the burned walls and furnishings, the conference room doorway, and Hitler's respirator, at left on the table, which was mentioned in the official Soviet report. This view also gives a good perspective as to the size of the men relative to that of the room. It is not really as small as the reports quoted above claimed! *SC*

(Above) This is a good outside view from the completed pillbox and ventilation tower (right), across the devastated New RC park, to the high wall just outside the french door of Hitler's palatial office at the middle left. His last troop review of Hitler Youth boys was held in front of that wall on March 30, 1945. This portion of the park is also where Hitler took Blondi for their walks. *SC*

(Right) A still scene from the 1948 Soviet postwar propaganda film, *The Fall of Berlin.* This scene was filmed at the actual site in Berlin, which was still a ruin. This reenactment shows the dead bodies of Hitler (right) and the late Führerin (left) being carried out of the bunker exit to a shallow ditch at far right to be doused with cans of gasoline and then set afire. Although it was SS Lieutenant Colonel Kempka and SS Major Gunsche who carried out the bodies with two SS enlisted men, it was SS man Hermann Karnau who actually burned the bodies steadily after chauffeur Kempka had set the corpses alight. Note the actor playing Dr. Göbbels (who supplied the matches) standing in the bunker exit at left, and the completed pillbox turret tower at the far right. *LC*

(Left) Here, Soviet NKVD secret police Chief Lavrenti P. Beria (left) and Foreign Minister Vyacheslav M. Molotov (center) have just emerged from their summer 1945 visit to the Führerbunker. At the left is the still-unfinished concrete pillbox turret tower. Winston Churchill and possibly a young John F. Kennedy—but not Stalin (so far as is known)—also came visiting that victorious summer of 1945. *LC*

(Below) A pair of Red Army soldiers (left) show five Allied war correspondents where the Hitlers' bodies were burned. Note the discarded jerry cans at left that were used to do the job. *SC*

Another view at another time of the same scene, with the unfinished tower at right and the Führerbunker exit at far left. Remarkably, the gas cans are still there and have not been carried off as souvenirs. On May 1, 1945, German Radio Hamburg made the following (untrue) announcement: "It is reported from FHQ that our Führer, Adolf Hitler, died this afternoon for Germany at his command post in the Reich Chancellery, fighting to his last breath against Bolshevism. . . . On April 30, the Führer named Grand Admiral Dönitz as his successor." After several reburials by the Soviets, the Hitlers' remains were taken to Moscow in 1970 for their presumed final destruction. *SC*

APPENDIX

List of Major Figures in the Book

Alfieri, Dino (1886–1966)—Italian Ambassador to Germany, 1940–43

Amann, Max (1891–1957)—Head of Nazi Party publishing house, Eher Verlag

Antonescu, Ion (1880–1946)—Rumanian Marshal and Head of State, 1940–44

Balbo, Italo (1896–1940)—Italian Air Marshal and Aviation Minister

Beck, Josef (1894–1944)—Polish Foreign Minister

Beck, Ludwig (1880–1944)—German General Staff Chief, 1934–38

Below, Col. Nikolaus von (1907–83)—Hitler's Air Force adjutant, 1937–45

Blaskowitz, Gen. Johannes (1883–1948)—Served in Polish and French campaigns (1944)

Blomberg, Field Marshal Werner von (1878–1946)—German Defense Minister, 1933–38

Bock, Field Marshal Fedor von (1880–1945)—German Army, commander in West and East

Bodenschatz, Gen. Karl (1890–1979)—Göring's liaison officer at FHQ

Bormann, Albert (1902–89)—Hitler's NSKK (Motor Corps) adjutant

Bormann, Martin (1900–45)—Reich Leader and Secretary to the Führer, head of the Nazi Party Chancellery

Bouhler, Philip (1899–1945)—Head of the Führer Chancellery, Berlin

Brandt, SS Dr. Karl (1904–48)—SS physician assigned to Hitler

Brauchitsch, Field Marshal Walther von (1881–1948)—Commander in Chief of the German Army (OKH), 1938–41

Brückner, SA Gen. Wilhelm (1884–1954)—Chief Adjutant to the Führer, 1933–40

Buch, Walter (1883–1949)—Chairman, Supreme Nazi Party Court

Group at FHQ Wolfsschanze: from left to right: Speer, Jodl, Guderian, Keitel, and Hitler. *Frentz*

Burgdorf, Gen. Wilhelm (1914–vanished 1945)—Chief of Army Personnel, 1944–45

Chamberlain, Neville (1869–1940)—British Prime Minister, 1937–40

Christian, Gerda Daranowski "Dara" (1913–97)—Hitler's secretary, 1937–45

Ciano, Count Galeazzo (1903–44)—Italian Foreign Minister, 1936–42

Daladier, Edouard (1884–1970)—French Premier, 1938–40

Darges, Friedrich (1913–)—SS adjutant to the Führer

Darre, Walther (1895–1953)—German Minister of Food, 1933–45

Dietrich, SS Gen. Josef "Sepp" (1892–1966)—Commander of Hitler's SS Bodyguard, 1933–38; Waffen (Armed) SS unit commander, 1939–45

Dietrich, Dr. Otto (1897–1952)—Reich Press Chief, 1933–45

Dönitz, Grand Adm. Karl (1891–1980)—Commander in Chief of the German Navy (OKM), Reich President as Hitler's 1945 successor

Eckart, Dietrich (1863–1923)—Hitler's first mentor

Eden, Sir Anthony (1897–1977)—British Foreign Secretary

Elser, Georg (1903–45)—Would-be assassin of Hitler, 1939

Engel, Maj. Gen. Gerhard (1906–76)—Hitler's Armed Forces adjutant

Epp, Gen. Franz Ritter von (1868–1946)—Nazi Governor of Bavaria

Esser, Hermann (1900–81)—Cofounder of the German Workers' Party and German State Secretary of Tourism

Fegelein, SS Gen. Hermann (1906–45)—Second SS liaison officer to FHQ for Himmler, 1943–45

Fiehler, Karl (1895–1969)—Nazi Mayor of Munich

François-Poncet, André (1887–1978)—French Ambassador to Germany

Franco, Generalissimo Francisco (1892–1975)—Chief of State of Spain, 1936–75

Frank, Hans (1900–46)—Minister of Justice, Governor-General of Occupied Poland

Frentz, Walter (1907–2004)—Hitler's Luftwaffe newsreel photographer for all FHQs, 1939–45

Freyend, Ernst John von (1909–80)—Keitel's adjutant

Frick, Wilhelm (1877–1946)—Minister of the Interior, 1933–43

Fromm, Gen. Friedrich (1888–1945)—Head of the Home, or Replacement (Reserve) Army, 1944

Galland, Adolf (1911–96)—Luftwaffe General of the Fighters, 1941–45

Giesler, Prof. Hermann (1898–1987)—Architect

Göbbels, Dr. Josef (1897–1945)—Nazi Propaganda Minister, Gauleiter (District Leader) of Berlin

Göring, Reich Marshal Hermann (1893–1946)—Commander in Chief of the German Luftwaffe, Reichstag President, designated successor to Hitler, 1933–45

Graf, Ulrich (1878–1950)—Early bodyguard for Hitler

Greim, Field Marshal Robert Ritter von (1892–1945)—Second and final Commander in Chief of the German Luftwaffe, and the last man Hitler promoted to field marshal

Guderian, Col. Gen. Heinz (1888–1954)—General Staff Chief, 1944–45

Gunsche, SS Maj. Otto (1917–2004)—Hitler's last SS adjutant

Hácha, Dr. Emil (1872–1945)—President of Czechoslovakia, 1938–45

Halder, Col. Gen. Franz (1884–1972)—General Staff Chief, 1938–42

Hanfstaengl, Ernst (1887–1975)—Nazi Party Foreign Press Chief until 1937

Heim, Heinrich (no dates)—Stenographer of Hitler's "table talk" at FHQ

Hess, Rudolf (1894–1987)—Deputy Führer, 1933–41

Hewel, Walther (1904–45)—Von Ribbentrop's liaison officer at FHQ, 1938–45

Heydrich, SS Gen. Reinhard (1904–42)—Founder of the Reich Main Security Office, Reich Protector of Bohemia and Moravia

Himmler, Reichsführer (RFSS) Heinrich (1900–45)—Head of the SS, 1929–45; Commander in Chief of Army Group Vistula, 1945

Hindenburg, Field Marshal Paul von (1847–1934)—President of the German Reich, 1925–34

Hitler, Adolf (1889–1945)—Führer and Reich Chancellor, Supreme Commander of the Armed Forces, Commander in Chief Army and Commander in Chief of Army Group A, 1933–45

Hoffmann, Prof. Heinrich (1885–1957)—Reich Photo Reporter

Horthy, Adm. Miklós (1868–1957)—Regent of Hungary, 1920–44

Jodl, Gen. of Artillery Alfred (1890–1946)—Chief of Armed Forces Leadership Staff, 1939–45

Junge, Gertrude "Traudl" (1920–2002)—Hitler's fourth and final personal secretary, 1943–45

Kannenberg, Artur (1896–1963)—manager of Hitler's homes

Keitel, Field Marshal Wilhelm (1882–1946)—Chief of the High Command of the Armed Forces (OKW), 1938–45

Kempka, SS Lt. Col. Erich (1910–75)—Hitler's chauffeur, 1936–45

Kesselring, Luftwaffe Field Marshal Albert (1885–1960)—commanded on all fighting fronts, 1939–45

Kleist, Field Marshal Ewald von (1881–1954)—served on Western and Eastern Fronts

Kluge, Field Marshal Gunther Hans von (1882–1944)—Commander in Chief West, 1944

Krause, Karl Wilhelm (1911–)—Hitler's first main SS valet, 1933–39

Krebs, Gen. Hans (1898–1945)—Last General Staff Chief, March 29–May 2, 1945

Kriebel, Gen. Hermann (no dates)—Leader of the Battle League, 1923

Krösigk, Lutz Graf Schwerin von (1887–1977)—Finance Minister, 1933–45

Kube, Erich (1887–1943)—Nazi Gauleiter (District Leader)

Lammers, Dr. Hans Heinrich (1879–1962)—Reich Chancellery Chief

Laval, Pierre (1883–1945)—Vichy French Foreign Minister, 1940–45

Linge, Heinz (1913–81)—Hitler's second and final SS valet, 1939–45

Lloyd George, David (1863–1945)—British Prime Minister during World War I

Lorenz, Heinz (1913–85)—FHQ Führerbunker Press Chief, 1945

Loringhoven, Freytag von, Baron Bernd (1914–)—Major, Operation Section, Army General Staff

Mackensen, Field Marshal August von (1849–1945)—Served in World War I

Manstein, Field Marshal Fritz Erich von (1887–1973)—Fought on Western and Eastern Fronts

Meissner, Dr. Otto (1880–1953)—Presidential Chancellery Chief, Ebert/Hindenburg/Hitler, 1923–45

Milch, Luftwaffe Field Marshal Erhard (1892–1972)—State Secretary of Aviation, 1933–44

Mohnke, SS Gen. Wilhelm (1911–2001)—Last Commander of Reich Chancellery Defense Group

Morell, Dr. Theodor (1886–1948)—Hitler's primary care physician, 1936–45

Mussolini, Benito (1883–1945)—Duce (Leader) of Italian Fascism, Prime Minister of Italy, 1922–43; head of Salo Republic, 1943–45

Neurath, Baron Konstantin von (1873–1956)—Hitler's first Foreign Minister, 1933–38

Oshima, Gen. Hiroshi (1886–1975)—Military Attaché and later Japanese Ambassador to Germany, 1933–45

Papen, Franz von (1879–1968)—German Reich Chancellor, Vice Chancellor, Ambassador to Austria and Turkey, 1932–45

Pavelic, Dr. Anté (1889–1957)—Poglavnik (Leader) of fascist Independent State of Croatia, 1941–45

Picker, Dr. Henry (no dates)—Stenographer of table talk at FHQ

Popp, Josef (no dates)—Munich tailor, Hitler's first landlord, 1913–14

Puttkamer, Rear Adm. Karl-Jesko von (1900–81)—Hitler's Naval Adjutant (OKM)

Raeder, Grand Adm. Dr. Erich (1876–1960)—Commander in Chief of the German Navy (OKM), 1928–43

Reichenau, Field Marshal Walther von (1884–1942)—Would-be Commander in Chief of the German Army

Ribbentrop, Joachim von (1893–1946)—German Ambassador to Great Britain, 1936–38; Hitler's second Foreign Minister, 1938–45

Richthofen, Field Marshal Wolfram von (1895–1945)—In charge of Stalingrad airlift

Röhm, Capt. Ernst (1887–1934)—SA Chief of Staff, 1931–34

Rommel, Field Marshal Erwin (1891–1944)—Commander in Chief Afrika Korps, 1941–43; Army Group B, France, 1944

Rosenberg, Alfred (1893–1946)—Minister of the Occupied Eastern Territories, 1941–44

Rudel, Col. Hans-Ulrich (1916–82)—Luftwaffe ace on the Eastern Front, destroyed 519 Red Army tanks and a battleship

Rundstedt, Field Marshal Gerd von (1875–1954)—Dean of the German World War II Marshalate

Schaub, SS Gen. Julius (1898–1967)—Chief Adjutant to the Führer, 1940–45

Schleicher, Gen. Kurt von (1883–1934)—German Reich Chancellor, 1932–33

Schmid-Ehmen, Prof. Kurt (1901–68)—Sculptor

Schmidt, Dr. Paul (1899–1970)—Chief Foreign Office Interpreter, 1933–45

Schmundt, Maj. Gen. Rudolf (1896–1944)—Armed Forces Adjutant, Chief of Army Personnel, 1939–44

Schörner, Field Marshal Ferdinand (1892–1973)—Last German Army Field Marshal appointed by Hitler in World War II

Schröder, Christa (1908–84)—Führer secretary, 1933–45

Schulze, Hans-Georg (1917–41)—SS adjutant to Hitler

Schulze-Kossens, Richard (1914–2000)—SS adjutant to Hitler

Schwarz, Franz Xavier (1875–1947)—Nazi Party Treasurer

Seldte, Franz (1882–1947)—Reich Minister of Labor, 1933–45

Simon, Sir John (1873–1954)—British Foreign Secretary

Speer, Albert (1905–81)—Hitler's second architect, 1931–42; Second Minister of Armaments and War Production, 1942–45

Spitzy, Reinhard (no dates)—Aide to von Ribbentrop in the Foreign Office

Steiner, Waffen (Armed) SS Gen. Felix (1896–1966)—Failed to rescue Hitler and Berlin, 1945

Strasser, Gregor (1892–1934)—Vice Chairman of the Nazi Party

Streicher, Julius (1885–1946)—Gauleiter of Nuremberg and Franconia

Stülpnagel, Gen. Karl Heinrich von (1886–1944)—Military Governor of Occupied France

Suñer, Serrano (no dates)—Spanish Foreign Minister

Todt, Dr. Fritz (1891–1942)—Hitler's first Minister of Armaments and War Production; his Organization Todt (OT) built all the FHQs, 1939–45

Troost, Dr. Gerdy (no dates)—Designed furniture for various Nazi Party buildings

Troost, Dr. Paul Ludwig (1878–1934)—Hitler's first architect

Wagener, Otto (1888–1971)—SA Chief of Staff, 1929–30

Warlimont, Gen. Walter (1894–1976)—Deputy Chief of Armed Forces Leadership Staff, 1939–44

Weber, Christian (1883–1945)—Early Munich Nazi

Weber, Dr. Friedrich (1891–1954)—Leader of Oberland Free Corps, Munich

Weidling, Gen. Helmuth (1891–1945)—Military Commander of Berlin, 1945

Weizäcker, Ernst von (1882–1951)—State Secretary in the Foreign Office, 1938–45

Wenck, Gen. Walther (1900–82)—Commander, Twelfth Army, like Steiner, also failed to rescue Hitler and Berlin in 1945

Wiedemann, Friedrich (1891–1970)—Hitler's WWI commanding officer; his NSKK (Motor Corps) adjutant, 1933–41

Wolf, Johanna (1900–85)—Hitler's senior secretary, 1930–45

Wolff, SS Gen. Karl (1900–84)—Himmler's first liaison officer with FHQ, 1939–43; Higher SS and Police Leader for Italy, 1943–45

Wünsche, Max (1914–)—Hitler's SS adjutant until 1940

Zeitzler, Gen. Kurt (no dates)—General Staff Chief between Halder and Guderian, 1942–44

SELECTED BIBLIOGRAPHY

Adam, Peter. *Art of the Third Reich.* New York: Abrams, 1992.

Baur, Hans. *Hitler's Pilot.* London: Miller, 1958.

Beierl, Florian M. *History of the Eagle's Nest: A Complete Account of Adolf Hitler's Alleged "Mountain Fortress."* Berchtesgaden: Plenk, 2001.

Below, Nikolaus von. *At Hitler's Side: The Memoirs of Hitler's Luftwaffe Adjutant, 1937–45.* London: Greenhill Books, 2001.

Bloecher, John, Jr. *Wolfsschanze 1998 Photos.* Baltimore: Danzig Study Group, 1998.

Carlson, Verner R. "The Hossbach Memorandum." *Military Review,* August 1983.

Cowdery, Ray R. *Grossdeutschland 1942: A Guide Book of Germany During the Third Reich.* Lakeville, MN: USM, Inc., 1992.

———. *Hitler's New German Reischschancel-lery in Berlin.* Kusnacht: Northstar Maschek, 1987.

Cowdery, Ray, R., and Josephine Cowdery. *The New German Reichschancellery in Berlin, 1938–45.* Rapid City, SD: USM, Inc., 2003.

Deming, Brian, and Iliff, Ted. *Hitler and Munich: A Historical Guide to the Sights and Addresses Important to Adolf Hitler, His Followers and His Victims.* Berchtesgaden: Plenk, 2000.

Dietrich, Otto. *Hitler.* Chicago: Regnery, 1955.

Domarus, Max. *Hitler: Speeches and Proclamations, 1932–45: The Chronicle of a Dictatorship, Volumes 1–4.* Wauconda, IL: Bolchazy-Carducci, 1990–2004.

Dresler, Adolf. "The Brown House, Germany." Berlin: Reich Committee for Tourist Traffic, 1935.

Fest, Joachim C. *Inside Hitler's Bunker: The Last Days of the Third Reich.* New York: Farrar, Giroux and Strauss, 2004.

———. *Speer: The Final Verdict.* New York: Harcourt, 2001.

Frank, Bernhard. *Hitler, Göring and the Obersalzberg.* Berchtesgaden: Plenk, 1989.

Frentz, Walter. *Führerhauptquartier Wolfsschanze 1941–45: Zeitgeschichte in Farbe.* Kiel: Arndt, 2001.

———. *Hitler's Berghof 1928–45/Zeitgeschichtes in Farbe.* Kiel: Arndt, 2000.

———. *Hitler's Neue Reichskanzlei: "Haus der Grossdeutschen Reiches" 1938–45, Zeitgeswchichte in Farbe.* Kiel: Arndt, 2002.

Gilbert, Felix. *Hitler Directs His War: The Secret Records of His Daily Military Conferences.* New York: Oxford University Press, 1950.

Göbbels, Josef. *My Part in Germany's Fight.* New York: Fertig, 1979.

Görlitz, Walter. *The German General Staff, 1657–1945.* New York: Praeger, 1962.

Guderian, Heinz. *Panzer Leader.* Cambridge, MA: DaCapo Press, 1996.

Halder, Franz. *Hitler as War Lord.* London: Putnam, 1950.

Heiber, Helmut, and Glantz, David M., eds. *Hitler and His Generals: Military Conferences, 1942–45/The First Complete Stenographic Record of the Military Situation Conferences From Stalingrad to Berlin.* New York: Enigma Books, 2002.

Heiden, Konrad. *Der Führer: Hitler's Rise to Power.* Boston: Houghton-Mifflin, 1944.

Henderson, Neville. *Failure of a Mission, Berlin 1937–39.* New York: Putnam's, 1940.

Hitler, Adolf. *Hitler's Table Talk, 1941–44.* New York: Enigma Books, 2000.

———. *Mein Kampf.* Boston: Houghton Mifflin, 1943.

Hoffmann, Heinrich. *Hitler Was My Friend.* London: Burke, 1955.

Hoffmann, Peter. *Hitler's Personal Security: Protecting the Führer, 1921–45.* Cambridge, MA: DaCapo Press, 2000.

Irving, David. *Hitler's War.* New York: The Viking Press, 1977.

———. *The Secret Diaries of Hitler's Doctor.* New York: Macmillan, 1983.

Joachimsthaler, Anton. *The Last Days of Hitler: The Legends, the Evidence, the Truth*. London: Arms and Armour Press, 1998.

Johnson, Aaron L. *Hitler's Military Headquarters: Organization, Structures, Security and Personnel*. San Jose: Bender, 1999.

Junge, Traudl. *Until the Final Hour: Hitler's Last Secretary*. New York: Arcade, 2004.

Kampe, Hans George. *The Underground Military Command Bunkers of Zossen, Germany: Construction History and Use by the Wehrmacht and Soviet Army, 1937–94*. Atglen, PA: Schiffer Military, Aviation History, 1996.

Kappes, Irwin J. "Hitler's Ultra-Secret Adlerhorst." MilitaryHistoryOnline.com, 2003.

Kaufmann, J. E., and H. W. Kaufmann. *Fortress Third Reich: German Fortification and Defense Systems in World War II*. Cambridge, MA: DaCapo Press, 2003.

Keitel, Wilhelm. *In the Service of the Reich*. New York: Stein and Day, 1979.

Kempka, Erich. *Ich habe Adolf Hitler verbrannt*. Munich: Kyrburg Verlag, 1947.

Kubizek, August. *The Young Hitler I Knew*. New York: Tower Publications, 1964.

Langsam, Walter C. *Historic Documents of World War II*. Princeton, NJ: Van Nostrand, 1958.

Large, David Clay. *Where Ghosts Walked: Munich's Road to the Third Reich*. New York: Norton, 1997.

Lehrer, Steven. *Hitler Sites: A City-by-City Guidebook (Austria, Germany, France, United States)*. London: McFarland, 2002.

———. *The Reich Chancellery and Führerbunker Complex: An Illustrated History of the Seat of the Nazi Regime*. Jefferson, NC: McFarland, 2006.

Le Tissier, Tony. *Berlin: Then and Now*. London: After the Battle, 1992.

———. *The Reichs Chancellery and the Berlin Bunker: Then and Now*. London: After the Battle, 1988.

———. *The Third Reich: Then and Now*. London: After the Battle, 2005.

Linge, Heinz. *Until the Fall*. Munich: Herbig, 1980.

Lorant, Stefan. *Sieg Heil! An Illustrated History of Germany From Bismarck to Hitler*. New York: Norton, 1974.

Lower, Wendy. *Nazi Empire-Building and the Holocaust in Ukraine*. Chapel Hill, NC: University of North Carolina Press, 2005.

McGee, Mark R. *Berlin: A Visual and Historical Documentation From 1925 to the Present*. Woodstock: The Overlook Press, 2002.

Melchior, Ib, and Brandenburg, Frank. *Quest: Searching for Germany's Nazi Past/A Young Man's Story*. Novato, CA: Presidio Press.

O'Donnell, James P. *The Bunker: The History of the Reich Chancellery Group*. Boston: Houghton-Mifflin, 1978.

Raiber, Richard. *Führer-Begleit-Battalion: Frontgruppen*. Hockessin, DE: unpublished manuscript.

Rhodes, Richard. *Masters of Death: The SS Einsatzgruppen and the Invention of the Holocaust*. New York: Knopf, 1992.

Schram, Percy. *Hitler: The Man and the Military Leader*. Chicago: Academy Chicago Publishers, 1999.

Seidler, Franz W., and Dieter Ziegert. *Hitler's Secret Headquarters: The Führer's Wartime Bases From the Invasion of France to the Berlin Bunker*. Mechanicsburg, PA: Stackpole Books, 2005.

Shirer, William L. *Berlin Diary: The Journal of a Foreign Correspondent, 1934–41*. New York: Bonanza Books, 1984.

Smith, Herbert Norton. *An Uncommon Man: The Triumph of Herbert Hoover*. New York: Simon and Schuster, 1984.

Speer, Albert. *Inside the Third Reich: Memoirs*. New York: Macmillan, 1970.

Stahlberg, Alexander von. *Bounden Duty: The Memoirs of a German Officer, 1932–45*. London: Brassey's, 1990.

Sweeting, C. G. *Hitler's Personal Pilot: The Life and Times of Hans Baur*. Washington, DC: Brassey's, Inc., 2000.

Taylor, Blaine. *Guarding the Führer: Sepp Dietrich, Johann Rattenhuber and the Protection of Adolf Hitler*. Missoula: Pictorial Histories Publishing, 1993.

Taylor, Telford. *The Breaking Wave: The Second World War in the Summer of 1940*. New York: Simon and Schuster, 1967.

———. *The March of Conquest: The German Victories in Western Europe, 1940*. New York: Simon and Schuster, 1958.

———. *Sword and Swastika: Generals and Nazis in the Third Reich*. New York: Simon and Schuster, 1952.

Toland, John. *Adolf Hitler*. Garden City: Doubleday, 1976.

Thomas, Hugh. *The Murder of Adolf Hitler: The Truth About the Bodies in the Berlin Bunker*. New York: St. Martin's Press, 1995.

Trevor-Roper, Hugh R. *Blitzkrieg to Defeat: Hitler's War Directives, 1939–45*. New York: Holt, Rinehart, and Winston, 1964.

Turner, Henry Ashton, Jr. *Hitler's 30 Days to Power, January 1933*. New York: Addison Wesley, 1997.

Warlimont, Walter. *Inside Hitler's Headquarters*. New York: Praeger, 1964.

Westwood, David. *German Infantryman (1), 1939–40*. Oxford: Osprey, 2002.

Zduniak, Jan, and Klaus-Jurgen Ziegler. *Wolfsschanze und Hitlers andere Kriegshauptquartiere*. Karolewo, Poland: Karolewo, 1998.

INDEX

ABOUT THE AUTHOR

Blaine Taylor is the author of seven books on the history of the Axis Pact powers before and during World War II. He also writes for *Military Heritage, Military Machines International*, and *Militaria International* magazines. A former U.S. congressional press aide on Capitol Hill, Taylor has won six awards for his writing and editing, and he appeared on the History Channel's *Automaniac* series, *The Cars of World War II*. A combat veteran of the U.S. Army 199th Light Infantry Brigade in the former Republic of South Vietnam during 1966–67, Taylor was awarded twelve medals and decorations, among them the Combat Infantryman's Badge (CIB). He lives in Towson, Maryland.